CAMARO

Text by Bill Holder and Photography by Phillip Kunz

MBI Publishing Company

First published in 1995 by MBI Publishing Company, PO Box 1, 729 Prospect Avenue, Osceola, WI 54020-0001 USA

The information in this book is true and complete to the best of our knowledge. All recommendations are made without any guarantee on the part of the author or Publisher, who also disclaim any liability incurred in connection with the use of this data or specific details.

We recognize that some words, model names and designations, for example, mentioned herein are the property of the trademark holder. We use them for identification purposes only. This is not an official publication.

MBI Publishing Company books are also available at discounts in bulk quantity for industrial or sales-promotional use. For details write to Special Sales Manager at Motorbooks International Wholesalers & Distributors, 729 Prospect Avenue, PO Box 1, Osceola, WI 54020-0001 USA.

Library of Congress Cataloging-in-Publication Data

Holder, William G.
    Camaro/Bill Holder, Phil Kunz.
        p. cm.—(Enthusiast color series)
    Includes index.
    ISBN 0-7603-0092-5 (pbk.)
    1. Camaro automobile—History.   I. Kunz, Phillip.
    II. Title. III. Series.
    TL215.C33H65   1995
    629.222'2—dc20   95-5978

On the front cover: With its bright all-red color combination and slotted headlight covers, this '69 RS is a real looker. This beautiful first generation Camaro, which is equipped with a 350ci/300hp engine, belongs to Roy Boyles.

On the frontispiece: The detail of the headlight covers of the '69 RS.

On the title page: Considered by most as the classiest of many classic Camaro designs, the first generation models—as characterized by this '67 Super Sport—was about as good as it got.

On the back cover: For 1968, the SS received a few subtle changes to its classic style. The most noticeable of these was the "big engine" hood. It featured two metal inserts that simulated carburetion stacks. Tony Burk of Dayton, Ohio, is the owner of this fine '68 Super Sport.

Printed in Hong Kong

Contents

Acknowledgments

Dr. Peter Gimenez—Dana experience
Mick Price—COPO/ZL1 expertise
Tom Boyd—Camaro collection
Ed Cunneen—COPO Connection
US Camaro Club
Ohio State Highway Patrol—Lt. Randell Meek
Bob Haynes—Z28 expert
Cover car owners—Roy Boyles, Tony Burk

Car owners—Melvin Butler, Gary Zembo, Rusty Symmes, Pam and Tom Brown, Bruce Coberly, Steve Gillen, Jim Wirth, Ted Cridts, Bryon Bonham, Harold Lunsford, Ken Marshall, Jeff Bertsch, Joe Estes, and Jim and Debbie DeHart.
Photography—All photography by Phillip Kunz unless otherwise noted.

Foreword

Every year, hundreds of different car models are sold around the world; most of which serve as transportation for a limited time and then fade into obscurity. But occasionally, a particular car will catch the attention of automotive enthusiasts as soon as it is introduced. Even more rarely, some of these models will survive as a part of the vehicle manufacturer's new car line-up for many years, undergo styling changes, and perhaps even grow in popularity. But few cars have been as popular and successful in so many ways as GM's Chevrolet Camaro.

Popular with drivers young and old when it was introduced in 1966, the Camaro quickly became a sensation at drag strips and circle tracks all across the land. Customizers, hot rodders, and car show entrants immediately fell in love with the new long-hood, short-trunk look and the versatile F-body chassis that accepted any Chevy drive train and huge rear tires without modification.

Today, the Camaro is still a popular attraction at drag races, cruise-ins, restored-car trophy competitions, circle track races, road rallies, custom car shows, pro-street events, and the salt flats. Probably no other car in history has appeared in so many car magazines. Perhaps best of all, the Camaro (now in its fourth generation) is still enjoying popularity on Chevrolet dealers' showroom floors.

In the golden days of grand classic autos, such as Duesenberg, Auburn, and Stutz Bearcat, only the very rich could afford super performance cars. But today, the common person in his or her Chevrolet Camaro can enjoy performance and automotive styling second to no car on the road.

Jim Wirth
Founder and former President, United States Camaro Club
Founder and former Publisher, *CAMARO CORRAL Magazine*
Founder, Auto Restoration Market Organization (ARMO)
Board Member, Specialty Equipment Market Association (SEMA)

CHAPTER 1

The Beginnings

Roots of This Famous Pony Car

So just what exactly is the Camaro? When it comes right down to it, it fills many voids. To some, it is a sports car, while others look at it as a muscular performance machine, while still others view it as a way to get through morning traffic driving to work and not taking up much room in a parking place.

Actually, though, the Camaro was, and is, all of the above. But in this book, we'll be looking more at the performance aspects of the machine. And with the Camaro, there is lots to talk about through the years. Even during the late 1970s and early 1980s, when the performance had gone away, the racy looks of the models still gave the appearance of multiple ponies under the hood.

No matter how the particular customer looked upon the reasons for making a Cam-

A number of high-performance versions of the early Camaros were built, such as this 1969 Yenko which carried a 427 big block powerplant.

aro purchase, there was certainly one heavy motivating reason from Chevy's point of view. The event took place in April 1964, three years before Camaro's introduction, when rival Ford introduced the super-successful Mustang. Not only was the Mustang a dynamite looker, it also had the performance to go with that look.

After all, it was the start of the muscle era, and the timing for the Mustang, with its 289 HiPo mill, couldn't have been better for Ford. Obviously, it couldn't have been worse for the Bowtie folks.

The sporty Ford product was successful beyond all dreams, with over 100,000 selling in its early months. So what did Chevy have to respond with? Absolutely nothing! There were thoughts about modifying the boxy Chevy II. But what was finally selected was the use of the projected 1968 Chevy II, which used conventional suspension geometry, unibody construction, and enough engine bay volume to tote the projected big-block engines. Fortunately for General Motors (GM), the project worked.

The Camaro project during its early days would carry the name of Panther, under the guidance of Pete Estes. He would later select the Camaro nametag, moving back to an old Chevy habit of naming their models starting with the letter "C". Camaro is a French word meaning "companion."

There is a point of clarification which should be made when discussing the earlier models. The case was that the Z/28, SS, and

The Camaro has been honored four times through the years as the pace car for the Indy 500. It happened the first year of its existence with this beautiful '67 pacer.

RS models weren't actually models at all, but options of the standard Sport Coupe. The options were so popular, though, that they took on a "model" identification with buyers.

There have been four Camaro generations through the years. The first, which would last only three model years, started with the initial 1967 model. The second generation reached to the second year of the 1980s; it was an era which saw performance drop off greatly. The third generation, which was another decade in length, saw the Camaro gain performance respect again in both appearance and under-the-hood aspects. The fourth generation, which began in 1993, continues the beat, and during the mid-1990s, shows no tendancy of slowing down.

Those first three models all carried basically the same body design, but the company did its job well, and suddenly the Camaro was a legend in its own time. The success was needed, though, because there was a lot of catching up to do with the streaking Mustang.

During that time period, Chevrolet flooded the market with a montage of models, both big- and small-block powerplants, transmissions, rear ends, and options that allowed potential buyers to basically build their own machines. The introduction of the Z/28, SS, RS, and a pair of Indy Pace Car models kept the Camaro name in front of the buying public.

During 1969, the performance world was set completely on its tail with the introduction of the awesome COPO Camaro model which carried the 427ci mill. Certain dealers also built their own modifications including Yenko, Dana, Nickey, and the Baldwin Motion.

The second era covered a dozen years, from the 1970 through the 1981 model year. Boy, did things change! The style moved from the boxy style of the 1960s to a softer, more aerodynamic look. It was also the period which saw the muscle era reach its peak, and then see the word "performance" become a bad word. The Camaro would also experience the trends.

The 1970 model would still see the 396 big block and a superb-performing 350ci/360hp powerplant. From there, though, it was all downhill in performance. The push was toward better handling, and, of course, fuel economy. After all, this was the period of long gas lines of the oil crunch.

During the period, both the SS and RS options went by the wayside, and the Z28 was gutted of its performance, the punchy 302 powerplant long gone. It goes without saying that if performance was your bag, you were certainly glad to see this era end. By the end of this "downgrade era", the Z28 was showing a sickly 175 net horsepower rating, which made the model a Z in name only.

Thank goodness, things started to change in the pony department with the start of the third generation (1982–1992). The era started off right when Camaro was named the Indy Pace Car. Accompanying this new beginning was a complete sheet metal redesign. Weight was down, and power was up during the 1980s with the horsepower figure back up to 190 for the 1983 Z28.

In 1985, Tuned Port Injection and the classy IROC-Z continued Camaro's return to performance respectability. In 1991, the ILE road racing package became the standard for the handling-minded. With the new 350ci/ 275hp powerplant, there was also an awesome six-speed transmission.

The RS became a separate model in 1989 for the first time. Also during this era was the introduction of the so-called B4C

The late 1980s were typified with the classy IROC-Z versions which evolved from the race series.

Special Service Package, an option built specifically for police use. It was first available in 1991 in RS Coupes only.

The beat continued in the fourth generation (1993 to the present). The Corvette-style LT1 powerplant was now in the Camaro, and performance (big-time performance!) was back in vogue. There were also the powertrains and suspension systems to go along with the impressive power figures. It was appropriate that the 1993 Camaro should be selected as the Indy Pacer.

Performance is back in the 1990s for this classic pony car in a big way. It's made differently these days—small blocks and electronic fuel injection versus the earlier big cubic inches.

But the results are the same—the Camaro is getting the job done in a huge fashion with no indications that the trend will stop.

Early Camaro Engine Associations

	302[1]	327[2]	350[3]	396[4]	454[5]
Sport Coupe	—	1967–69	—	—	—
Super Sport (SS)	—	—	1967–72	1967–72	—
Z/28	1967–69	—	1970–74	—	—
COPO	—	—	—	—	1969
Yenko	—	—	—	—	1969

[1] Includes 290hp version
[2] Includes 210 and 275hp versions
[3] Includes 295, 300, 270, 360, 330, and 200hp versions
[4] Includes 325, 350, 375, and 240hp versions
[5] Includes 425, 430, and 450 horsepower versions. (Dealer-installed 427s were also available in 1967 and 1968 with Yenkos and other dealer versions.)

There was no questioning the identification of the '69 Z. The emblems were carried on the grille, rear panel, and fenders. There was also that distinctive hood striping which was carried the length of the car.

CHAPTER 2

The Z Cars

Small Block Pizzazz of the Z/28 and IROC-Z

It looked like a race car just sitting there, and there was good reason for the similarity. In order to go Trans-Am racing, it was necessary to be "holomogated", or have a minimum number of street versions of the race car produced. Thus, the Z/28 Camaro was born, and with the exception of only two years, has been on the Chevy marque ever since. The Z/28, interestingly, was just an option until 1977.

The initial 1967 Z/28 was previewed to the press in November 1966, but only 602 of the model would be produced that first model year. It was somewhat subdued, with pinstriping being the only side body detailing. Broad racing stripes, which meshed nicely with the slotted Rally Wheels, swept over both the hood and rear deck. The model probably fooled many as being a plain Camaro without the hood scoops, body stripes, and flashy badges. In fact, the first Z didn't even carry the Z/28 identification.

To go with the deceptively docile look, Chevy engineers did themselves proud with a high-revving 302ci mauler that was actually a destroked 327. Internals were almost full-race with a forged steel crankshaft, 11:1 compression heads, and an amazing 800cfm Holley carb. The horsepower was rated at a laughingly low 290hp, a figure that was quoted to ease insurance rates for high performance cars of the period.

In an era when big block powerplants were getting all the publicity, the Z/28 powerplant was acquiring its own enthusiasts and contesting with the Mustang 289 Hi-Po powerplant. The engine was capable of 7500rpm with no valve float and capable of 14.9sec/97mph quarter mile performance.

The Z/28 was actually an option of the line which required an extra $358.10. Included in the package besides the engine were a pair of deep-tone mufflers, heavy-duty front and rear suspension, heavy-duty radiator, quick ratio steering, 3.73:1 rear axle, and the special stripes. It probably goes without saying that this model is one of the most desirable of all the Camaro collectables. It also goes without saying that if you wanted creature comforts like air condition-

AIR INDUCTION

BOLD NEW STRIPING AND
HOOD SCOOP DESIGN MAKE
Z28 LOOK AS GOOD AS
IT PERFORMS.

SOLENOID-OPERATED COLD AIR INTAKE DUCT
HELPS ENGINE BREATHE WHEN IT NEEDS IT MOST.

VENTED, POWER-ASSISTED
FRONT DISC BRAKES.

AVAILABLE CAST-ALUMINUM WHEELS
WITH WHITE-LETTERED STEEL-BELT
RADIALS IN SIZE P225/70 R-15.
THEY HELP THE HUGGER HUG.
(TIRES SUPPLIED BY VARIOUS MANUFACT

Z28 SPRINGS OFFER EXTRA
DEFLECTION: 365 LBS/INCH
IN FRONT, 130 IN REAR.

SHOCKS PROVIDE THE DAMPING YOU NEED
THANKS TO SPECIAL Z28 VALVING. 1" PISTON.

FRONT AIR DAM, REAR SPOILER AND FLARED FENDERS
GIVE YOU THE GOOD LOOKS YOU EXPECT FROM A "Z".

Z28

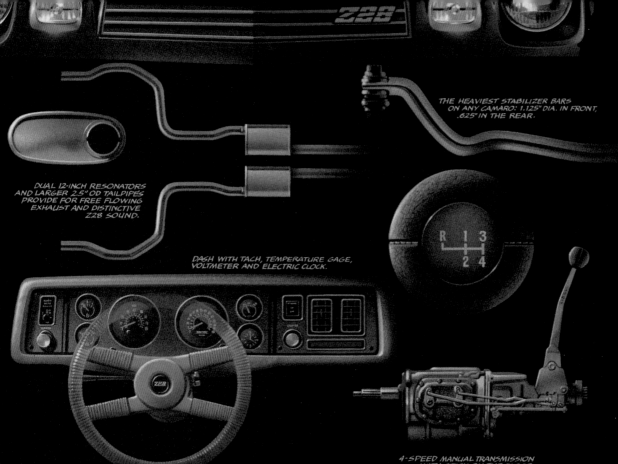

THE HEAVIEST STABILIZER BARS ON ANY CAMARO: 1.125" DIA. IN FRONT, .625" IN THE REAR.

DUAL 12-INCH RESONATORS AND LARGER 2.5" OD TAILPIPES PROVIDE FOR FREE FLOWING EXHAUST AND DISTINCTIVE Z28 SOUND.

DASH WITH TACH, TEMPERATURE GAGE, VOLTMETER AND ELECTRIC CLOCK.

4-SPEED MANUAL TRANSMISSION WITH STICK ON THE FLOOR. (AUTOMATIC REQUIRED IN CALIFORNIA.)

CHEVY CAMARO Z28 FOR 1980.
THE ENGINEERING OF A DRIVING LEGEND.

What you see here is part of the heart of a Camaro Z28...the components that make it very special, extremely capable, a driving legend. It's engineered, from the ground up, with the most sophisticated suspension in the Camaro line, with special shocks, anti-sway bars and springs to help stabilize the ride. It's equipped with steel-belted radials. Bold new cast-aluminum wheels are available in three colors. There's a four-speed gearbox that delivers the power from the smooth 5.7 Liter V8 engine.* A new solenoid-operated air induction scoop helps the engine breathe. The exhaust sings through dual resonators. The Z28 bristles with a good-looking front air dam, fender flares and a rear spoiler.

The Camaro Z28 for 1980. It's your turn to own a driving legend. Buy or lease one today.

5.0 Liter (305 Cu. In.) V8 with available auto. trans. only in California.

CHEVY CAMARO. THE HUGGER.

Chevrolet

ing and an automatic transmission, you had better forget about the Z/28!

The November 1966 Chevy national advertisement for the new Z/28 described its qualities to the hilt: "The Z/28 package was developed to make the Camaro an exceptional touring machine having relatively light weight, a smaller but highly responsive V-8 engine with four-speed transmission, and suspension refinements that result in excellent stability and handling characteristics."

In retrospect, you would have to admit that the initial Z/28 was a greatly misunderstood car upon its introduction. But there

Previous page
The Z28 for 1980 was a fantastic looking machine set off by its macho triple racing stripe. Although power was not its strong suit, you'd never have known that from the design.

There it is, the pony car that set the public on its ear, the 1967 Z/28. With only 602 produced that first year, it's a significant collectable in the 1990s. *Chevrolet Photo*

was a method in design engineer Vince Piggins' philosophy. He wanted a machine that would qualify for the Trans-Am series. The engine that evolved was a combination that used the 283 engine's 3.00in stroke crankshaft combined with the 327 engine's 4in bore cylinder block.

There is really no monumental reason how the Z/28 got its catchy designation. Quite simply, 28 was the next number in line after the Z27 Super Sport Option, which would use the SS designation.

For 1968, the Z/28 was no longer a secret; 7,199 were sold—over ten times the

The standard powerplant for the 1968 Z/28, as it had also been for the previous year, was this 302ci/275hp hustler which was an integral part of the Z/28 ($400.25) package.

1967 total. It was getting to be more of a drag on the pocketbook with the cost now just topping the four hundred dollar figure. "Refinement" would have to be the best descriptor of what was accomplished to the second Z/28.

Appearance changes were the vacuum-operated headlight cover doors, side marker lights, and an optional RPO-D80 rear spoiler. A wheel hop traction problem was addressed with the second Z when a rear traction bar was added.

The punchy 302 mill was still in place. But to really light your fire, a Cross Ram intake manifold with dual four-barrel Holley Carbs could also be ordered; it was estimated to add 50hp. The Cross Ram unit, interestingly, had to be installed by the dealer. Reportedly, 125 were constructed, making them a rare find indeed in the 1990s.

The complete redesign that was accomplished on the second-generation Z is certainly evident in this photo. The most obvious difference is in the centered grille and separate headlights. It certainly gave this model a completely different look.

There were also three optional Special Performance Packages which were provided. The packages consisted of (1) plenum air intake with special air cleaner and duct system, (2) special exhaust header, and (3) a combination of both. Find an original of any of these setups, and the value goes through the roof. The production of these packages, though, was discontinued before the end of the model year.

This Z would also pick up the factory option of four-wheel disc brakes, along with the COPO-style cowl induction hood which could also be ordered. The price of the Z/28 Package was now sitting at $473.25.

But for that getting-serious money, you were getting serious performance equipment including dual deep-tone mufflers, heavy duty suspension and radiator, temperature-controlled fan, and the 3.73:1 ratio axle. If

For the by-far-most-plentiful of the first generation Z/28s, the '69 version retained the popular 302 powerplant. This, though, would be its final year succumbing to a 350ci mill the following model year.

you added special exhaust headers, the cost spiraled to $779.40, and if you also added the plenum air intake, expect to lay down $858.40. It sounded like a lot of coin for the time, but remember, you were effectively getting a full-race street racer.

Z/28 number three in 1969 continued to show the love of the public for performance as the production billowed this year to 20,302. The fact that the model won the Trans-Am racing championship with the Penske team doing the honors for the second straight year certainly didn't hurt the love affair.

The '69 Z picked up a bit of a macho look with sheet metal modifications to the complete sides including doors, rear panels, and rear quarters. Recall that the Camaro

For the performance-minded, the Cross Ram induction system was a must. The extra carburetor provided additional top-end horsepower. *Trae Prado Photo*

A Trans-Am Z-Car

This particular '69 Z/28 is one of the most interesting in the land because of the multitude of options it carries.

This car, just like the Mark Donohue Trans-Am race version, is equipped with the two four-barrel carburetors mounted on a Cross Ram induction manifold. That extra carburetor created lots of top-end horsepower and demonstrated greater flexibility near the top of each gear and a higher top speed.

The carburetors are 600cfm Holley four-barrels. The engine put out 290hp at 5800rpm along with the same figure of lb-ft of torque at 4200rpm.

Other features of this particular car include a special instrument option which placed the ammeter, temperature, oil pressure, and fuel gauges in stacked pods on the console. On the dash, the speedometer and tach filled the large squares above the steering wheel. Finally, there is the RPO JL8 four wheel disc brake option that puts the final icing on the cake.

(Bob Haynes provided the information on this fabulous rare Z/28.)

was still sharing its side sheet metal with the Firebird, a situation that would continue for a number of years.

The 1969 model year was the final year of the classic initial design, and many consider the model the best of the Camaro breed. If that '69 you have in your possession just happens to be a Z/28, then you've got a step up. The Z package price increased twice during the model year ending at a $522 figure.

Some 200 buyers of the '69 Z thought it was worth the investment to plop down an additional $500 for the optional four-wheel disc brakes. The car magazines at the time gave the innovative brake system a thumbs up. There was even a mimeographed instruc-

23

tion manual that described how to construct a roll cage for a road racing Camaro.

Enter the 1970 model year; it was officially called the '70 1/2 Camaro, and you'd have a hard time recognizing the Z/28 or the Camaro itself. The Camaro had been completely redesigned, and the Z had acquired many additional changes itself.

To start off with, a very subtle change involved the actual changing of the Z designation from Z/28, which had been carried on the sheet metal through the '69 model, to the new Z28 designation. Why the deletion of the "/"? Nobody seems to know. Whatever, from here on out, we're calling it the Z28 too.

But to the performance-minded Z buyer, the biggest change by far was that the long-standing 302 powerplant was gone for the 1970 model year. However, they needed not lament as the ponies were up by a mauling 70 horses with the infamous LT1 350ci mill pounding down 360hp! It was basically the Corvette powerplant with minor changes. The 70-1/2 Z was also the first to have the Turbo Hydra-matic available, as a new camshaft allowed the addition of the automatic.

Also coming with the Z package were front and rear swaybars, heavy-duty springs, and standard front disc brakes.

To go with the new performance capabilities, the Z sheet metal was completely remodeled into what some enthusiasts consider the best ever of the Z breed. Gone was the characteristic body-width grille; new was

a centered snout grille with the lights located outside. The new look was more racer-like, and with the Z's wide dual hood and rear deck striping, it was even more intensified.

The new powerplant used cylinder heads incorporating 2.02in intakes and 1.60in exhausts and a forged crankshaft. The aluminum intake manifold was continued with a closed plenum style for this unit.

It's amazing, though, that only 8,733 of the model were sold. A rare and super-desirable collectable in the 1990s to be sure!

The muscle era was on the downturn in 1971, and the Z28 350ci mill (now called the Turbo-Fire 350) felt the brunt with a 30hp jab at its former 360 capability. The downgrade came from the compression ratio downgrading to a lowly 8.5:1. Appearancewise, the '71 Z didn't change much with the front air dam being standard along with a larger rear spoiler.

The fact that the racy spoiler package was no longer a part of the 1972 Z28 told even more vividly of the turn away from performance. But that trend was even more evident under the hood where the Turbo-Fire had been gutted to a paltry 255nhp. The model carried a 3.73:1 Positraction rear end and special suspension, but the Z28 was quickly becoming more of an appearance package instead of a performance model. Production was only 2,575.

The 1973 Z28 became domesticated with the first availability of air conditioning (with automatic transmission). Ten more horses escaped from under the hood, and the solid lifters were replaced by hydraulic units. The long-standing aluminum intake was now fabricated of cast iron. Even with the performance spiral continuing, there was a significant upturn in production with a five-fold increase to 11,574.

The 1974 Z hardly deserved that last-letter-of-the-alphabet designation that had meant so much performancewise in its earlier days. They called it Sport Suspension this year instead of Heavy Duty Suspension. The performance G80 Positraction Rear Axle was included with the Z package, but only 6,473 of the 13,802 Z buyers took advantage of it. Thankfully, the horsepower value didn't stray any further downward, staying at the 245 figure.

Then, for two years, the Z28 completely dropped out of the Camaro option book. Gone, but was it finished for good? For two model years, that was the case, but Chevy engineers brought it back in with renewed prestige.

Although it was late getting off the starting line in the 1977 model year, it was a model in itself as opposed to being just an option. Known as RPO IFQ87, there was still a 350ci powerplant in place, but there was hardly V-8 performance in place with only 185 horses. The Z28 was the only model in which you could acquire the M21 four-speed, but only about a third of the 1977 buyers made the selection.

The Z28 that model year was a bad third in sales (14,349) among the three models sold, the other two being the Sport Coupe and Type LT Coupe. Performance was practically a nasty word during this time with all the national advertising pushed toward the Z's outstanding handling characteristics.

In 1978, the Z's horsepower was still at 185, even though the model was dynamite-looking on the exterior. In 1980, however, the horsepower trend turned the other way with the introduction of the RPO LMI 350ci/190hp powerplant; 45,137 sold.

The 1982 Z28 was a dynamite seller, with almost 70,000 sold, a total which included the Indy Pace Car version. It was the start of the third generation with completely new body shaping.

New ponies were under the hood of the '83 Z—the RPO L69, which punched 190nhp with a Rochester four-barrel, an aluminum intake manifold, and dual snorkel air cleaner. Performance was getting back in style. In 1984, there were over 100,000 Z28s sold, and the retail price was now up to $10,620.

In 1985, there was another Z in the Camaro camp, the so-called IROC-Z, an option model derived from the International Race of Champions race series. Not a separate model, the IROC-Z was an appearance option of the Z28 for this model year. The IROC was characterized by the large IROC-Z decals on the lower door position.

The IROC-Z option was continued through the 1990 model year, but that would be the final IROC since Chevy did not renew the International Race of Champions contract for 1991.

But the option did prove popular

through its six years with 1986 being the best sales year with 49,585 being sold.

A Z28 convertible was available in 1987 with 744 being sold. The big news for 1987, though, was the RPO B2L 350 powerplant which belted out 225hp with iron heads.

The Z28 was gone for 1988 with the IROC-Z (now a separate model-IFP87) being the only last-letter model for the year. Both the RPO B21 and LB9 engines were available with the model.

In 1989, Chevy introduced the "ILE" option, developed for the SCCA Showroom Stock racing series. In order to acquire the package, it was necessary to order the RPO G92 with the IROC-Z. Included in the RPO was four-wheel disc brakes, dual converter exhaust system, oil cooler, 145mph speed-

The complete redesign that was accomplished on the second-generation Z is certainly evident in this photo. The most obvious difference is in the centered grille and separate headlights. It certainly gave this model a completely different look.

ometer, and 5500rpm redline tach. The package was available with the 350ci (RPO B2L) or 305ci (RPO LB9) powerplants, with 230hp and 195hp, respectively.

In 1991, the Z28 came back with a performance vengeance, 478 of which carried the ILE equipment. It was the third straight year for the performance package and was coined with the RPO G92 nomenclature. The package could be ordered with either the 305ci LB9 V-8 (205hhp) with a five-speed transmission or the 350ci B2L with an automatic.

In 1992, the ILE package was in place again (705 sold), and again it was available only with the Z28. We were definitely back in the performance era again with 245hp from the top-gun RPO B2L engine, a figure it had sported since 1990.

In 1993, the Z28 continued to see improvements to the suspension system with a multi-link system with two trailing arms and a 19mm stabilizer bar. The magic LT1

There was no mistaking the new 350ci/360hp powerplant for the l970, or the 1970-1/2 model as the company called it. Atop the shiny air cleaner, the red decal told of the killer performance directly beneath.

nomenclature also came on line that year, a similar 350ci powerplant that powered the Corvette. With the Vette, the powerplant was rated at 300 horses, but it was 25 less with the Camaro.

The LT1 carried through with the Z28 the following two years. In 1995, the mill came with the optional Acceleration Slip Regulation (ASR) system which increased handling and traction control.

The dash design for the '70 Z28 was both functional and beautiful.

Rated as one of the best-looking Z28s ever, this '79 model displays the low front spoiler and body-length striping.

The IROC-Z was the second Z name as demonstrated by this 1987 IROC. The name came from the IROC series which used a number of identically prepared Camaros with drivers from several national racing series.

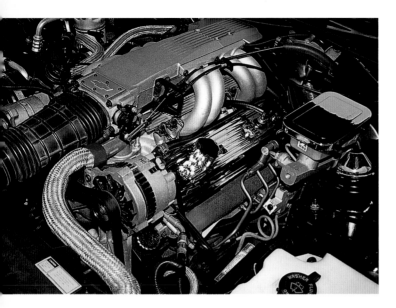

Performance was starting its return in the 1990s. Here, this punchy LB9 305ci provided 205 horses.

The 1994 Z28 had a design that cut through the wind. Note that the Z28 emblem is blocked out in black letters.

This dazzling '69 RS convertible really shows its
stuff. The $458.15 option attracted 20,302
buyers.

CHAPTER 3

Super Sport and Rally Sport

Stripes and Big Block Performance

It was a hard choice to make during those early years, whether to buy the Trans-Am race-derived Z/28, the Super Sport (SS), or Rally Sport (RS) models. A lot of buyers opted for the latter pair, which could also be simultaneously ordered on the same Sport Coupe.

The SS was available with the Camaro its very first year, and if performance was your game, you had to love this option. But for the really big horsepower numbers, you had to wait a bit during the model year. When the SS package was first introduced, it was only possible to order the L48 350ci engine, which produced 295hp.

But that would all change mid-year with a pair of 396ci big blocks (the L35 punching 325hp and the L78 with even 50 more than that) being available. There were 4,003 of the 325hp 396 and even less of the 375hp mauler at 1,138. Maybe it wasn't surprising on the latter since the buyer had to plunk down an extra $500.30 for the ultra big ponies.

The L48 350 mill was power enough, though, for many Super Sport buyers as the 295hp version sold 12,476. Although not available with the SS option, mention should be made of the L30 327 powerplant, available in both 1967 and 1968, which produced an impressive (and many times unnoticed) 275hp.

But there was much, much more with the SS option, both from the performance and appearance areas. With the former came a dynamite suspension system to put the big horsepower to the pavement. There were also the heavy duty engine mounts for the big blocks, along with a heavy-duty rear axle and clutch.

The SS emblems seemed to be everywhere on the body, sitting in the middle of the black-out grille, gas filler cap, and the front quarters. But when the 396 was ordered, the front quarter SS badge was replaced with a special 396 Turbo Jet emblem located directly under a block Camaro nametag. Throw in the custom hood, black-out rear panel, and SS striping, and this was one killer machine from just about any angle you looked at it.

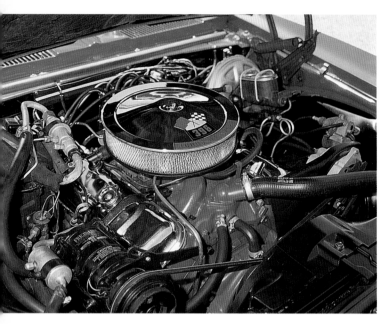

The magic numbers for the SS and RS models in 1967 were 396ci. This was the lowest horse-power version of the killer mill, the L35, which carried a 325hp rating.

If your desire for the looks of your Camaro was a little more sedate, then the so-called Rally Sport (RS) was for you. The RPO Z22 added only $105.35 to the sticker and was strictly an appearance option.

Included with the RS were valance-mounted parking lights, side moldings, black stripes, gutter moldings, electrically operated headlight doors, special grille, and black painted taillight bezels. The RS identification was obvious with RS emblems on the front quarter, gas cap, and radiator grille.

Now get this! If you really wanted to deck out the first Camaro, you could order both options on the same model. But when

The Z22 Rally Sport Package was a popular choice during its initial year (1967) with almost 65,000 delivered.

The interior of the '67 RS really got your attention.

that happened, the RS got the short end of the stick with no RS emblems to be found.

In addition to both Sport options, you could also keep kicking up the price of this first Camaro with a whole horde of additional options.

The popularity of the SS and RS models continued in 1968, but there were some subtle changes made. You definitely had to look closely to observe them.

First, instead of the SS emblem embedded in the vertical bumblebee stripes, the 350 or 396 engine displacement numbers were used. Also, the SS emblem was moved to the front fender position located below the new SS stripe and directly under the Camaro nametag. And finally, there was the so-called "big engine" hood, which featured

When you combined the 1967 SS and RS options, you came up with the killer SS/RS model shown here. Immediately evident externally were the vivid SS striping and the RS's black-out grille.

twin metal inserts each carrying four simulated carburetion stacks.

For the Super Sport's second year, there was a third 396 powerplant (the L35) available whose horsepower was halfway between the already existing 325hp and 375hp models. In addition, for the ultimate performance enthusiast, there was the so-called L89, a special 396 mill equipped with aluminum heads, larger valves, and a custom Holley Carb. Introduced later in the model year, only 272 were built. We are talking very rare and desirable for the collector. There was also a potpourri of transmissions available with four four-speeds and a pair of automatics.

The Rally Sport continued pretty much unchanged from the first year and remained

It was interesting that Chevy elected to announce the RS for 1967 in lower case letters. Different, but it sure got your attention.

a popular option with 40,997 constructed. It was again possible to order both the SS and RS together.

The final year of the first generation, 1969, saw the popularity of the GM pony car billow to 243,085. Camaro year three looked a lot like its earlier cousins, but there were some refinements with slightly altered sheet metal sporting sharp bends and curves. A lot of Camaro fans were indeed sorry to see this design fade away with the complete redesign of the following year.

It was again a year of performance with the three 396 engines (the L34, L35, and L78 396 motors) being optional fare for the Super Sport. These muscular powerplants carried the RPO chambered exhaust option. The standard powerplant was the L48 350ci/300hp mill which would become a popular engine choice in the years of its existence.

Pizzazz and style would have to be the descriptors of this '67 SS/RS convertible interior.

This particular '67 SS/RS was special ordered by a Chevy executive at the time and is loaded to the hilt with options.

That super-rare and super-powerful L89 was still available in 1969, but only 311 customers checked off the option. Not surprising, since that engine option cost an additional $710.95, which was about one-fourth the cost of the basic Camaro model.

The Super Sport option was identified by RPO Z27 with the L48 being the standard powerplant with the package. It required an extra $295.95 to procure the impressive package which this year included front discs, heavy duty suspension, the custom hood backed by insulation, wide oval tires, blackout and bright accents, detailed engine compartment, and the expected SS badges. (A limited number of Super Sports of this era were either factory- or dealer-converted with 427ci powerplants. These so-called COPOs and other mutations are covered in the following chapter)

The 1970 model year saw big changes, but it took a while to get things going before the new body style was introduced. Therefore, the new machine wasn't introduced until February of 1970 and was called the 1970-1/2 Camaro. For many, the wait was worth it while others still yearned for the first generation styling.

The L78 was the top guy 396 for the 1968 model year. The mill provided 375hp with 4,575 making the purchase.

The design changes for the first of the new Camaros were significant with a completely new look. The full body-wide grille was gone and replaced with the centered rectangular design with the headlights now located outside the grille.

The Super Sport version sold only 12,476, but recall that it wasn't available for a full model year.

The standard 1969 powerplants were available with the initial models, but the available L48 350ci/300hp was also greatly

There were considerable differences between the rear ends of the '68 SS (left) and the '69 RS.

Note the differences between the rear lens designs.

admired. That impressive mill sported a 10.25:1 compression ratio and 380lb-ft of torque. A *Road & Track* road test showed a moderate capability of 86mph and 16.6sec in the quarter mile. Although this powerplant is sometimes referred to as the same powerplant as the Corvette LT1, that was NOT the case.

A number of the Chevy big and intermediate models in 1970 got the big block 454, and there was consideration that the Camaro would also be a recipient of the powerful mill, but it was not to be, even though there were a number of dealer-installed units.

It was possible to purchase an interesting combination of the RS and Z/28. When purchased, both emblems were carried on the front quarters as shown here. A unique order to be sure.

The headlights were visible in the '68 SS design. When the RS option was checked, headlight covers were added. There were those that liked both designs.

The 300hp 350 was a part of the Super Sport option which also included special accents, power brakes, hood sound insulation, black-out grille, and SS emblems on the rear deck, grille, and front quarters.

The RS package was again available in 1970, both with or without the SS package, and included a custom grille and a montage of appearance options. The RS could be ordered with both the SS and Z28 options, and was selected by 27,136 buyers, more than twice the number that took the Super

Several different nose-striping techniques were available with the '68 SS models. This half-stripe arrangement was one of them.

Camaro's New Super Scoop:
It's like frosting on the frosting.

Basic ingredients, Camaro SS, The Hugger: 300-hp 350 V8. Wide oval treads on 14 x 7 wheels. Beefed-up suspension. Power disc brakes. A floor-mounted 3-speed shifter.
   Extra topping you can order: A new Super Scoop hood that shoots cooler air to the carburetor for an added dash of dash.
   The whole setup works off the accelerator. You step on the gas, it steps up top end power.
There you have it: Super Sport with Super Scoop.
Add you and stir.

CHEVROLET
Putting you first, keeps us first.

The cowl-induction hood was performance personified. Chevy called it the "Super Scoop" and indicated that the hood provided an "added dash of dash." It was just one of the performance options that could be ordered with the '69 Super Sport.

Tony Burk of Dayton, Ohio has one of the best and most highly optioned '68 Super Sports in the country.

Again in 1969, the 396 powerplant was the top gun mill. This is the 325hp version of the big block.

Next page
The interior of the 1969 RS was flashy to say the least. This particular model sports a rare all-red interior/exterior color scheme.

Sport. It could well have marked the start of the downturn of performance.

The '71 Camaro was pretty much a duplication of the previous year with only minor changes. The downturn in performance was evident with thirty horses (or 10 percent of the previous year's 300hp value)

being clipped off the standard Super Sport L65 L350ci powerplant. A 396 (actually it was 402ci) could be ordered (the LS3) with 300 nhp available. But, only 1,533 took the option.

The Super Sport option, costing $313.90 this fourth year, (with 8,377 buyers) includ-

The 1969 Camaro SS keeps tough company.

For two out of the last three years it's been chosen the official Indy 500 pace car. Check one out and you'll know why.

Engine choices start with a 300-hp 350 V8 and work their way up. For more power, a special new intake hood is available. We call it Super Scoop. It opens on acceleration, ramming huge gulps of air to the engine.

Additional credentials: beefed-up suspension, white-lettered wide ovals on 14″ x 7″ wheels, power disc brakes and a special transmission with floor shift.

It takes a lot to get this crowd started. That's why Camaro SS sets the pace.

For competition to follow.

Putting you first, keeps us first.

Camaro SS...and friends.

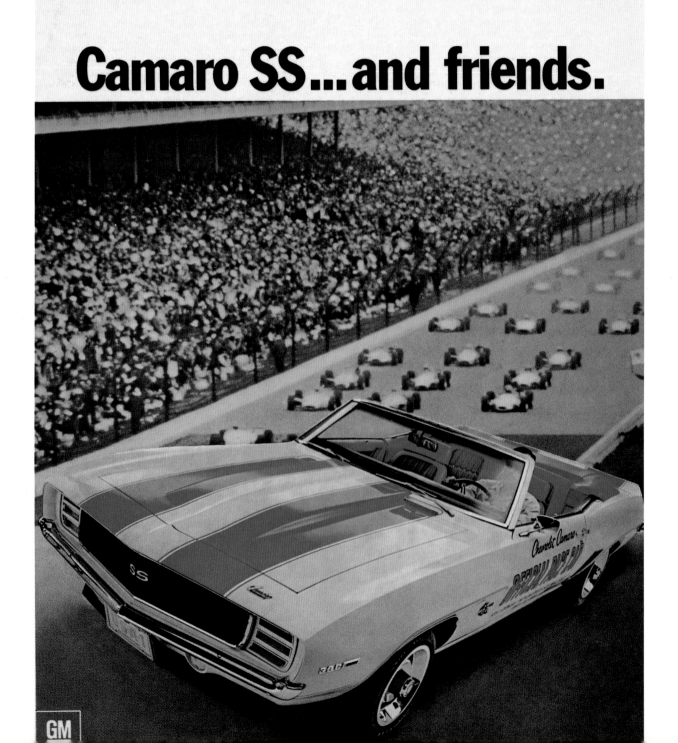

The RS interior for 1969 still looks good in the 1990s.

Previous page
Chevy sure didn't mind using the selection of the Camaro as the Indy Pace Car as an advertising bonanza. Being selected to lead the field on Memorial Day really showcased the '69 model.

ed, in addition to the L65 powerplant, power brakes, bright accents, dual exhausts, blackout grille, special trim, and remote mirror, with only a pair of SS emblems on the steering wheel and front quarters. The still popular RS (this year costing $179.05) had 18,404 buyers.

The Super Sport and Rally Sport were still on the option books for the 1972 Camaro, along with the same engine choices as the year before, but the horsepower was continuing to spiral. The L65 was still the standard Super Sport powerplant, but its ponies had dropped like a rock to the two hundred level. The optional LS3 396 powerplant was now down to only 240hp.

Big changes took place for the 1973 model year as the long-standing Super Sport option departed in favor of the Type LT, a model which could be combined with the Z28, Rally Sport, or even both at the same time. The LT was available from 1973 through the 1978 model year.

The LT was different from the Super Sport option it replaced in that it was a completely separate model, RPO IFQ87. There were a pair of 350 powerplants available, the L48 and L65, which had 175hp and 145hp, respectively.

The Rally Sport departed in the 1974 model year as the power levels continued their downward trend. The performance-minded hung their heads during the remainder of the 1970s and into the 1980s. Interestingly, the RS became a separate model in

New Camaro. **Now our competitors know how the captain of the Titanic felt.**

You're going to find that a lot of Camaro's new appeal lies below the surface.
It begins at the very bottom. With our completely new advanced-design suspension. It's helped make Camaro's already-precise ride even more precise. To let you drive the car. Instead of vice versa. (Everybody knows how to build a suspension. We know how to make it work.)
Front disc brakes are standard on all models. There are six engines available all the way up to the Turbo-Jet 396 V8 with 350 hp. Four transmissions including a special 4-Speed for the Z28. A wide stable tread. The protec-

tion of side-guard beams.
Inside, a new instrument panel. And new seats. Two buckets in front. Deeply contoured. To hold you in place through the tightest maneuvers. And in back, two semi-buckets that do the same for your friends.
And, of course, we haven't even touched on Camaro's sleek new appearance. You've got eyes. These are just a few of the reasons why our competition is on edge. They've run into something they can't quite handle.
New Camaro. The Super Hugger. Putting you first, keeps us first.

See it, Feb. 26th. At your Chevrolet Sports Dept.

Camaro Sport Coupe with Rally Sport equipment.

The Camaro was completely redesigned for 1970 as was flaunted by this advertisement. The mid-year introduction gave the Camaro, the Rally Sport here, a completely new look.

1978, actually the Type LT Rally Sport Coupe.

The 1980 model year would be the final RS for a number of years, with the emblem not appearing on the sheet metal for the 1981 through 1986 model years. In 1987, there was a limited edition RS option offered in California before the RS came back nationally in 1988.

The RS has been a popular seller through the late 1980s and into the 1990s, far exceeding Z28 sales.

Although only an appearance package during its early days, it's interesting that the RS took on much more of a performance aura in recent years. Starting in 1990, the so-called RS Coupe was a completely distinctive model which could be fitted with the optional 305ci/170hp RPO L03 powerplant.

In 1992, 589 RSs were equipped with the Special Service Package (RPO B4C), a police package, which provided a combination of handling and performance enhancements. Either of two potent setups, the 350ci B2L

This factory photo was one of the first of the completely redesigned Rally Sport for the 1970 model year. *Chevrolet Photo*

The 350ci powerplant was capable of 255bhp in the 1972 models.

with automatic, or the 305ci LB9 with a five-speed, could be ordered. Also included in the $3,479 package ($4,309 with RPO B2L) were 16in wheels, 145mph speedometer, engine oil cooler, custom suspension, and four-wheel disc brakes.

The 1980 Rally Sport was little changed from the previous year and featured the classy molded-in rear spoiler.

CHAPTER 4

Special Editions

COPO, Yenko, Dana, Baldwin-Motion, & Nickey; Modern; and Concept

Granted, through the years, it has long been possible for the Camaro performance enthusiast to build his dream machine. But during the late 1960s and early 1970s, there were some dream machines—some beyond belief—assembled by the factory and certain dealerships. Most were awesome 427 powered machines that were, quite simply, the ultimate!

In the early 1990s, it started happening again with some machines where stock Camaros were taken and given their own performance and handling tweaks. There have also been a number of special performance machines factory-built for police use. And finally, through the years, there have

Relive the Yenko days of old with its 1990s counterpart. Here's the killer DRM/400 Camaro that carries a DRM 400 Series LT1 engine displacing 383ci and pumping out 430 boiling ponies. Everything else about the hauler has been modified to make this a killer aftermarket Camaro. The old days are back, big time!

been a number of concept vehicles built which emphasized appearance more than performance. Here's the story of these interesting Camaros.

COPO Camaros

Chevy first responded to the call for more performance by constructing two special COPO (Central Office Production Order) versions in 1969. Approximately 500 Camaros were produced under COPO 9561 and equipped with cast iron block 427ci mills that produced an advertised 425hp.

But then it got even better. There were also sixty-nine outrageous COPO 9560 427 all-aluminum ZL1 430hp screamers built. Guess it goes without saying that those horsepower values were conservative at best. There were those that said the ZL1 was more in the neighborhood of 500 ponies!

The real company motivation for the creation of such powerplants was to have Chevy running up front in national Super Stock drag racing. The COPOs definitely answered the call. If you should ever come across a real

COPO, it's an investment that's as good as a blue chip stock.

Right off the bat, the models were almost totally unidentified on the sheet metal. For some reason, Chevy decided that there would be no fancy stripes or blackout treatment. The models could have just as easily been carrying six-cylinder engines if you didn't notice a couple subtle badges. The 427 numerals which were carried on the hood of the 9561 model were the only indication that its L-72 powerplant and associated powertrain equipment were putting down the big horsepower.

There was certainly no announcement of what was under the hood of the '69 COPO Camaro.

"Plain Jane" would be the best way to describe the exterior of this magnificent hauler.

The L-72 mill sported a four-bolt main block, 11:1 forged aluminum pistons, mechanical camshaft, and a forged steel crank. Topside, a monstrous Holley 780 carburetor sat atop an aluminum intake manifold. Cooling was aided by an RPO V48 Harrison Heavy-Duty four-core radiator while the engine compartment was topped by the RPO ZL2 ducted hood assembly which hooked up directly to the carb.

Other RPO options included power front disc brakes with either a four-speed manual or the Turbo 400 automatic. There were also the RPO F41 high performance suspension, a twelve-bolt differential and multi-leaf springs, heavy-duty shocks, and a special

The '69 COPO was truly a factory super car, the interior of which is shown here.

4.10 Positraction with heat-treated ring and pinion.

The ZL1 version was also externally austere with no external indications of the fire that breathed under the ZL2 hood, which didn't even announce the 427 displacement numbers, the only possible hint of blinding performance. With the higher ups of General Motors frowning on the building of such "unsaleable" models, Vince Piggins—head of Chevy's Product Promotion Department—worked a deal with drag racer Dick Harrell and dealer Fred Gibb.

The amazing aspect of the aluminum COPO engine was that the option priced out at an out-of-sight $4,160, made even more

You want power and performance? No problem with the COPO 9561 mill with 425 pounding ponies. The aluminum ZL1 version added an additional 5hp.

unbelievable when you consider that the basic '69 Camaro base price was just over $2,700! The other powertrain and suspension options were identical to the 9561 option.

The ZL1 engine featured the aluminum block with cast iron cylinder sleeves, aluminum heads, and other aluminum components bringing the weight down to a trim 500 pounds. Later versions of the powerplant would carry the 850cfm Holley Carb. Figuring a power-to-weight ratio, you would have to admit that you were taking a full race powerplant in every sense of the name.

The COPO number for the ZL1 427 version was 9560, magic numbers indeed for this highly collectable factory muscle car.

There were rumors that factory dyno data showed the horsepower to be in the area of 585hp. With slicks, the ZL1 was capable of high 11sec performance in the quarter mile. Was the ZL1 the ultimate Camaro? It would be difficult to argue that it wasn't.

Yenko Camaros

But the COPO story didn't end with just the factory involvement with these perfor-mance machines. A number of dealers wanted to fashion their own versions of the 9561 with their own personal touch.

The cars modified by high performance dealer Don Yenko are the most famous of the 427-powered Camaros. In fact, Yenko was deriving 427 machines before they came into being as COPO factory versions. He accomplished the 427 modification during 1967 and 1968 and identified the conversions with a flashy set of performance decals

Aluminum block and heads were the name of the game for the ZL1 427 powerplant. You want performance? You got it big time here!

cascading over the body. Reportedly, there were 54 conversions in 1967 and ten more in 1968.

The main identification came from the Yenko/SC nomenclature embedded in the body-length stripe along with an outrageous hood stripe design.

With the success Yenko had in selling his 427 cars, he made an agreement with Chevy to purchase a number of the 1969 427 COPOs which had the big mill already installed.

The first modification run of the those Yenko machines took place in the January-through-May 1969 time period where a Stewart Warner tach was bolted onto the instrument column. Later versions would use the factory tach with a 6000rpm red-line and a top end capability of 7000rpm.

And if you really wanted to make your Yenko more racy, there were a number of additional options that could really light your fire. For some significant extra dollars

The initial Yenko Camaros carried dealer-installed 427 iron block powerplants. This is a '68 version.

you could have added SW gages, Doug Thorely headers, Atlas aluminum wheels with the Yenko logo on the center caps, power steering, and a Hurst dual-gate shifter for the automatic-equipped cars.

As a rule, Yenko Camaros came rather sparsely optioned, but many buyers would opt for a number of appearance options including vinyl roof, factory instrumentation, exterior style trim group, console, special front bumper, and special interior group. You could also order a striking five-spoke Torque Thrust-style wheel that really set off this hauler.

But it again was the stripe detailing that really distinguished these brutes. Besides the full-length body stripe, there was the hood which carried a pair of wide dual strips on the raised portion. They terminated with a front facing arrow with the sYc nomenclature, for Yenko Super Car, of course.

There were only six colors available with the Yenko, but they were all flashy—Lemans Blue, Fathom Green, Rally Green, Olympic Gold, Daytona Yellow, and Hugger Orange. There is some conjecture about the number of '69 Yenkos built, with the best estimates being an initial order of a hundred. But the

The Yenko installation of the 427s during 1967 and 1968 gave the appearance of a factory setup. For the 1969 models, the cars would come to Yenko with the 427s already installed.

orders Yenko received quickly overwhelmed that number so he reportedly put out an additional 101. Of the 201 built, a great majority (171) were four-speeds.

Unlike the factory COPOs, Don Yenko wanted to flaunt that 427 powerplant, and as such, the magic 427 numerals were installed on the cowl position. Also, there was the characteristic Yenko badge located directly below the script Camaro on the lower front quarters. The emblem was also in place on the blackout rear deck panel. Another interesting change from the factory COPO was the horsepower decal on the air cleaner which announced 450 horses on the Yenko as compared to the 25 horse less value

With the distinctive striping all over the body, there was no mistaking the '69 Yenko Camaro.

on the factory versions.

The exploits of the Yenko Camaro were announced with a press release from Yenko on April 21, 1969. "So fast were the times turned in at York, PA on Saturday, April 19, set by a Yenko Camaro 427 that officials stopped the action for a clock check. The car turned the quarter mile in the unbelievable elapsed time of 11.94sec at 114.50 mph. The Camaro was wearing Goodyear 8in slicks on the rear, and a hastily installed set of headers." It's little wonder that the model was so effective on the nation's drag strips in the Super Stock class.

The rear of the '69 Yenko body stripe contains the embedded "Yenko" lettering in the rear of the stripe.

But, it should be noted, that even though the Yenko Camaros got most of the publicity, there were other Yenko conversions on Novas, Chevelles, and even some Vegas and Corvairs.

The factory data will tell you that the 1972 Camaro didn't have a 400ci powerplant, but don't tell Don Yenko who devised such a machine called the "Super Z." A limited number of these machines carried a 290hp version of the 400ci engine.

Baldwin-Motion Camaros

Numberwise, Yenko might have been the top dog in the Camaro special edition arena, but there were several other dealers doing their own thing. One such conversion was known as the Baldwin-Motion Phase II and III Camaros and were the products of Motion Performance Inc., an affiliate of Baldwin Chevy, a Long Island dealer.

With the late 1960s Baldwin-Motion mutations, the SS emblems were in place in their factory positions, in addition to "SS427" on the cowl hood. The actual engine change was accomplished by BM personnel, with "massaged" 427s being inserted in both the Phase II and III versions.

The BM II version used the dual-exhausted 450hp version hooked to a close ratio Muncie four-speed, Hurst shifter, special suspension with rewelded spring perches, and a Positraction rear end. The engine compartment sported a heavy-duty radiator, chrome valve covers and air cleaner, power front disc brakes, and a special ignition system. The

package retailed at a healthy $3,900.

If you wanted just a little more spark and fire, the Baldwin-Motion Phase III model featured a kicked-up 427, which was rated at 500hp and carried a unique three-barrel Holley Carb, and the so-called "Super-Bite" suspension. This killer engine also featured dual

"sYc" was the lettering that was located on the front of the flashy hood of the '69 Yenko Camaro. Standing for "Yenko Super Car," that was exactly what it was.

electronic fuel pumps, tuned headers, clutch fan, aluminum flywheel, and a Lakewood scatter shield.

Hard to believe that we're talking a street car here! You had to figure on an additional $1,100 over the Phase II for this model.

Since many of these cars were taken directly to the drag strip from the showroom, a number of buyers made some interesting orders for the cars. Motion cars have been seen with dealer-installed front tow hitches and side-mounted exhaust pipes.

How many of these rare machines were produced is unknown, but what is known is that there were also several other mutations including a basic SS 427 version, a souped-up SS 396, a Phase III SS 396, a hopped-up Z/28, and a Phase III Z/28. In 1970, it has been reported, that a 454 BM Camaro was assembled and sold by the performance dealership. We'd sure like to see one of those machines. You better believe that all these versions are extremely rare!

Also, in 1971, there was an awesome machine called the '71 Phase III 454 with a minimal 73 produced. This Motion creation

If you wanted abundant ponies, you sure got it with the Yenko 427 mill which provided 425hp.

began life as a 350 LT1 powered Z28, but that mill was removed in favor of the 450hp LS6 454. But that wasn't all. There was also every high performance goodie that the customer desired, like headers, traction bars, M22 four-speed, and a 3.73 Positraction. Supposedly, the machine was capable of 11sec quarter mile performance, and with those kind of components, that clocking would be hard to argue.

One of the designing geniuses behind the Motion cars was engineer Bill Mitchell. His philosophy was simple: build a street car that you could buy, take to a national drag meet, and win. And all you had to do was turn the key!

Dana Camaros

The name of this Camaro modification was the 427 Dana Camaro which was another dealer's attempt to add punch to the first two years of the Camaro breed. Probably all the cars being modified were SS models and best estimates indicate that

Another modification during the late 1960s was this version accomplished by Berger Chevrolet of Grand Rapids, Michigan.

about a hundred cars were modified.

Dana Chevrolet in South Gate, California, reportedly had eight bays set aside for this performance experiment. And interestingly, there was practically nothing externally that would alert you that a real street racer had pulled up to the light beside you. For the '67 models, there was a Dana emblem on the front quarter while the nomenclature was contained on the hood for the 1968 versions.

The Dana package contained the 427ci/ 425hp V-8 (with finned valve covers), heavy duty suspension, 6in wide steel wheels, a heavy-duty radiator, and four-speed tranny. Appearance components included the standard SS package, red stripe tires, a unique twin-scooped fiberglass hood, and the insignificant Dana emblem which was carried on some Dana models on the front quarter.

According to the Dana Registry, there were also Z/28 Danas. Again, the cars started out as factory SS350s which were converted to the Z/28 look.

Nickey Chevrolet of Chicago also produced some interesting 427 mutations. No missing that dealership decal with the reverse "K."

The July 1967 *Motor Trend* Dana road test article indicated that additional performance and suspension options could be ordered from the Dana boys. "Extras peculiar to this car are the three two-barrels, 435hp V-8 ($150), Stage I ($235) and Stage II ($275) suspension package—both for street use— and a Stage III package intended for racing."

Berger Camaros

"By Berger" on the rear valance was the only indication that this wasn't your standard Camaro. Berger Chevrolet in Grand Rapids, Michigan had long been in the performance business, but when the COPO and ZL1 hit the market, the organization had some Yenko-type ideas.

The modification took place on as many as 50 (exact number unknown) COPO machines ordered from Chevy which put the dealership in second place behind Yenko. Reportedly, half of the number were automatics and half were stick shifts. All came with the 140mph speedometer option which was part of the COPO 9737 Option. Berger, like Yenko, added the 450hp decal to the air cleaner. Remember, Chevrolet had continued to insist the value was the ridiculously low 425 value.

Of course, the customer could also order just about any other performance goody like engine tweaks, special suspension, and traction bars. The Berger Camaros also carried a front quarter stripe that terminated at the rear of the door edge.

Nickey Camaros

Another performance Chevy dealer, Nickey Chevrolet in Chicago, also used the 427 Camaro as a tool to enhance that high-performance image. Working with noted drag racer Dick Harrell, a number of 350-powered '67 models had their mills jerked, and the expected 427s inserted. The new powerplants were set back such that the front spindle and center of the number one piston aligned, a perfect weight balance for drag racing.

But the Nickey alteration just didn't leave the 427 alone; there were three-two and two-four carb setups available! You could also order a heavy-duty Hayes Clutch or the new Turbo Hydra-matic. The Nickey 427 also came with a standard 3.31 Positraction

It was known as the B4C Special Service Package and was available only to the men in blue. This is a 1993 version.

rear end, traction bars, and heavy-duty suspension. Quite frankly, this was not a machine for grocery getting, but a low 13sec quarter mile performer at an awe-inspiring 108mph category.

Externally, there was again little to designate the Nickey mutation other than a small Nickey emblem on the rear quarter and polished chrome mag wheels. The January 1967 *Tach* magazine named the Nickey Camaro as its Performance Car of the Year, "capable of challenging the MOPARs and Fords that are dominating the big block drag classes."

Harrell Camaros

There was also a collaboration between Fred Gibb Chevrolet in LaHarpe, Illinois and Harrell. This was the same dealership that had worked with Chevrolet engineers in the development of the ZL1 model. Harrell modified a number of Camaros, providing both new modified COPO machines and even modifying customers' used cars. The history and final disposition of these rare machines is somewhat clouded.

Other Muscle-Modified Camaros

There were other lessor-known dealerships doing their own Camaro muscle modifications. Reportedly, Alan Green Chevrolet in Washington State was such a dealer, and one of its reworks, a '68 SS, has been identified carrying an L88 427 powerplant.

There was also a one-of-a-kind Blue Max '67 mutation which was created by the race mastery of Roger Penske and Mark Dono-

hue. Undoubtedly, it was Sunoco Blue from their Trans-Am racing effort which also used Camaros.

Police Car Camaros

Muscle Camaros through the years have also played a part in law enforcement. It started in 1979 when the California Highway Patrol evaluated a dozen specially prepared Z28s as high-speed pursuit vehicles. The machines retained the factory spoilers and fender flares, but the expected police-associated equipment was added. The patrol's standard-issue shotguns were shortened to fit the Z's interior.

In more modern times, the Camaro returned to the Men in Blue line-up as the Special Equipment Option (SEO) B4C "Special Service Package." Available only to law enforcement, the machines were RS models equipped with the 350ci powerplant, 16in wheels, four-wheel disc brakes, limited slip rear ends, engine oil coolers, and heavy-duty electrical systems.

The B4C option continued through the 1995 model year with the 275hp LT1 350 powerplant with the choice of either a four-speed automatic or six-speed manual.

Modern Performance Conversions

As was the case in the late 1960s and early 1970s, it has also become the case again to acquire aftermarket performance Camaros. To say the performance levels of these machines is awesome is really putting it mildly.

Probably the best known of the companies doing this work is Callaway Competition with its so-called C8 Camaro. The model carries a 383ci/404hp powerplant and shows a 0-60 time of 4.8sec and an impressive 12.9sec quarter mile clocking. The impressive engine also produces 412lb-ft of torque and comes with a lifetime warranty. Callaway was also offering a custom CamAeroBody body design.

Doug Rippie Motorsports has also gotten into the Camaro upgrade business with its DRM 400-Series Camaro. The model is reportedly capable of 4.5sec 0-60 runs and a top speed close to 190mph. The package also offers a competition-style suspension system along with upgrades to the brakes and gear ratios.

Concept Camaro

Finally, the many concept Camaros through the years must be mentioned in the special edition category even though they each were one-of-a-kind cars. The concepts started in the 1960s and have continued through the years.

There have been such famous models as the Camaro Waikiki which featured wood-

The "Camaro Waikiki" concept car, using a first generation Camaro, featured wood-grain paneling and rectangular headlights. *Chevrolet Photo*

1984 was the year of the Olympics, and Camaro celebrated the event with a special edition.

grain paneling and rectangular headlights while the so-called Caribe had a pickup box instead of a trunk.

This cold black '94 model carries an interesting racing connotation. It's called the Dale Earnhardt Special and was accomplished by Elite Motor Coach of Dayton, Ohio. The modifications consisted of the custom leather seats, radical flair package, and the Dale Earnhardt seats.

Dazzling would have to be the description of the
'93 Indy Pace Car design.

CHAPTER 5

Pace Cars

On Show at the Brickyard

The Greatest Spectacle in Racing (i.e. the Indianapolis 500) has proved through the years to provide huge exposure to a particular automotive model through the month of May. The honor, of course, is the model's selection as the Indy Pace Car, and the national advertising windfall is unbelievable.

Camaro has had this honor four times, twice during the model's first generation (1967 and 1969), once at the very start of the third generation (1982), and once during the fourth generation (1993).

In addition to the pace car replicas that were produced each year, there were also three pace cars that were modified as the "real pace cars," the machines that would do the actual leading of the field at the start of the race. For Camaro, the first three pacers were modified for the pacing job with engine and suspension changes. With the '93 model, the changes were very minimal.

1967 Pace Car

It was appropriate that the Camaro would be so honored its first year, just as the Mustang competition had also been honored during its inaugural year. You can believe that Chevy really beat the drum in its national advertising campaign with that blue striped pace car standing tall.

That first pacer was certainly one macho-looking machine to accomplish that important buyer-attention job. First of all, the model selected for the Indy duty carried both the SS and RS trim options, 732 Interior Trim Code, factory-painted blue bumblebee stripe, and blue pinstriping. But, of course, it was the Indy decal identification that really set off the Ermine White hauler, lettering that almost completely covered each door. "Chevrolet Camaro" was scripted in gold, "Official Pace Car" was blocked out in blue while the bottom lettering was carried in black.

The numbers of that first Indy Camaro were extremely few in number (best estimates between 100 and 130) with about half (some 56) being at the track for the big race. The pacers carried both the 350ci and 396ci powerplants (the latter obviously being much more collectable to enthusiasts) while the three actual pacers were specially prepared.

At least one of those actual pacers (probably the one that actually paced the race) has been located. It's in the possession of Dan Young Chevrolet in Indianapolis. That trio of real pacers was modified with the RPO L35 396ci/375hp powerplant, the M40 Turbo Hydra-matic, and a 3.07 Posi rear end. Other changes included special tweaking of the engines, along with a heavy-duty battery and alternator.

1969 Pace Car

Surprise! The Camaro would pace the Brickyard only two years later; the first time in fifty years that the same model car would

A line-up of magnificent Camaro Indy Pace Cars, the 1967, 1969, and 1982 models.

do the pace duties in two of three straight years. Even more surprising was the fact that the body style hadn't changed appreciably.

But Chevy advertising wasn't complaining and would make the most of the opportunity, benefiting from the lessons learned just two years earlier. One thing was for sure, there would be many more replicas built; this year some 3,675 of the striking Hugger Orange and Dover White machines rolled out.

Chevy named the model the "New Camaro Indy Sport Convertible Option." It was constructed under Regular Production

It was appropriate that the Camaro, in its first year, would be honored as the official Indy Pace Car.

Option (RPO) Z11. Yep, for those Bowtie drag racing fans, that was the same code that had been used to identify specially modified 427 drag cars in the early 1960s.

As had been the case with the first Camaro pacer, the machine would again use both the SS (RPO Z27) and RS (RPO Z22) options. There would be changes in the

The interior of the '67 Indy Pace Car replica, along with the complete car, was used in national advertising.

striping, though, which would be applied in the Z/28 manner. The body sill was retained in white, the sport striping was removed, and the Hugger Orange fender striping was added.

Again, the pacer replicas could be ordered with either the 350 or 396 power-plants. The pacer was topped off with the ZL2 induction hood and the RPO Z17 wheels. Definitely, this was one tough-look-

The powerplant for the actual pace cars for that first Camaro year was a 396 powerplant, but it was a souped-up adaptation of the 375hp version. This is the actual motor of one of those "real" pace cars.

ing leader of the pack. A number of options could also be ordered to bring the replicas very close to the real pacers.

The 396ci/375hp big block was again the selection for the actual Brickyard performer and was hooked up with a Turbo 400 and a twelve-bolt Posi rear end. There were also the RPO JL8 disc brake option and 15in rally wheels.

1982 Pace Car

It would be thirteen years before Chevy's premier pony car would be honored again at the Brickyard. And the '82 pacer would be a monumental-looking machine. The big change, obviously, was that this pacer would be blue instead of the white the pacers used the first two times.

The detailing was done in red and silver

The 1969 Indy Pace Car was again Camaro, and the color scheme was completely different with orange being the predominant detailing color.

with the seats having silver vinyl with blue cloth inserts. Also, there was a red stripe on the aluminum wheels with Goodyear Eagle GT radials.

Power was more than adequate with the 305ci engine available with either a cross-ram fuel injection arrangement or a Rochester four-barrel. The 165hp rating for the fuel injection version was twenty-five higher than the carbed model.

The pace car replicas were loaded to the hilt with a three-speed automatic hooked to

Here, a pair of '69 Camaro pace cars show both their front and rear faces. Note that the cars are dominated by the wide twin stripes that cover both the hood and rear deck.
David Tucker Photo

a 3.23:1 rear end. Also, there were the AM/FM radio, quartz clock, special instruments and tach, sport mirrors, rear spoiler, leather steering wheel, deluxe luggage compartment, and Z28 options.

With those minimal horsepower values, you can probably guess that the real pacers had to have some considerable souping up. That's a good assumption, because the actual race leaders carried aluminum 350ci mills with four-bolt mains, steel cranks, and LT1 cylinder heads. The mills perked at 11:1 compression ratios and sported a 250hp rating at 4600rpm.

The lettering on the '69 pace car was almost identical to the two-year-earlier pacer, the biggest difference being that the orange color was used instead of blue with the '67 model.

The real pacer engine also sported a cross-ram injection unit and aftermarket Cyclone AR headers with special mufflers. The model also carried the needed 140mph speedometer, the approximate speed that was required for the on-track duties.

Exactly how many of this model were produced is not exactly certain, but the best estimates are about 6,300.

You better believe that orange was the predominant color in the '69 pace car interior, as can readily be seen from this view.

1993 Pace Car

A testament to the performance capabilities of the '93 Z28 was certainly in place when NO engine modifications were required for the model to be an Indy Pace Car! Therefore, the on-track cars were practically identical to the pace car replicas.

The only additions to the real pacers included the strobe lights, roll bar, safety harnesses, and on-board fire extinguishers.

The lack of a hopped-up engine is understandable since the 275hp LT1 small block was under the hood. It was hooked to a four-speed automatic transmission.

The graphics on the '93 pacer really set off the machine. The body was actually a two-toner with the top portion being a dark shade with white coming on the bottom por-

It would be a tough choice to choose between this pair of early Camaro pace cars. For sure, the 1967 pacer is a lot rarer as only about 100 were produced.

tion. Red and yellow striping separated the colors with the Indy door lettering in red, yellow, and light green.

The earlier Camaros are getting harder and harder to find. So if you want a Camaro pace car, you better grab up one of these newer muscular pacers.

A two-tone blue and silver motif was the highlight of the 1982 Indy Pace Car. The Indy identification lettering was much smaller on this model than on the earlier two pace car designs.

CHAPTER 6

On the Track

Strip, Oval, and Road Course Camaros

In many Camaro fans' minds, this classic pony car was born to race, and that's exactly what it's done in many realms through its almost three decades.

The list of drivers who have wheeled Camaros through the years reads like a Who's Who with the likes of Mark Donohue, A.J. Foyt, Mario Andretti, Al Unser, David Hobbs, Bill Jenkins, and Scott Sharp, just to name a few. Here's a brief look at some of the Camaro's numerous successful racing ventures.

Trans-Am Racing

Probably the highlight of the Camaro in Trans-Am racing occurred in its early years with the incomparable Roger Penske directing its fortunes. With Mark Donohue at the wheel, there were ten victories in twelve outings including a streak of eight straight. The following year, in a battle with the Parnelli Jones Mustang team, a second championship was accomplished. Camaro teams achieved their 25th T-A victory in July 1973.

A decade later in 1983, Camaro came back on the scene again winning ten of twelve races with Camaro drivers David Hobbs and Willy T. Ribbs finishing first and second in the drivers championship. More recently, Scott Sharp brought Camaro dominance into the 1990s with titles in 1991 and 1993.

Oval Track Racing

The Camaro was the machine of choice during the 1970s and 1980s with national-level short track series', such as ASA, ACT, ARTGO, NASCAR All-Pro, and others. Also, the Camaro proved that it could also dominate on the longer tracks winning the USAC Stock Car National Championship in both 1978 and 1979 with one A.J. Foyt at the wheel.

Camaros dominated the ASA circuit in the 1980s. Here, Joe Shear gets it on at the Queen City Speedway in Cincinnati in 1985. *David Tucker Photo*

A '68 Penske Trans-Am racing Camaro, completely restored and running the vintage circuits, brings back the good old days of the 1960s. *Spencer Lane Photo*

A pair of racing Camaros, the early Penske T/A car on the right and the modern Scott Sharp machine on the left, bracket a 1992 25th anniversary model. *Chevrolet Photo*

International Race of Champions (IROC) Series

The International Race of Champions was one series where the Camaro was always the winner. From 1974 through 1989, this TV series matched a dozen of the world's best drivers in twelve equally prepared Camaros.

Bobby Unser won the first IROC title in 1975, followed by Foyt's titles in 1976 and 1977. The original fleet of production-based models was then replaced by tube-framed replicas built by stock car specialist Banjo Matthews. Al Unser, Mario Andretti, and Bobby Allison would then win the next three titles.

Discontinued in 1980, the series started up again in 1984 when 20 racers were assembled by Jay Signore. Carrying 420hp V-8 mills, the high-tech racers could really put

One of the most recognizable racing Camaros is this 1979 model which just happened to be the ride of one A.J. Foyt in USAC competition.

on a show. In six years, stock car drivers won the title four times with Cale Yarborough, Harry Gant, Geoff Bodine, and Terry La-Bonte taking the honors.

IMSA/SCCA Showroom Stock

For the amateur racer with a Camaro, the SCCA Showroom Stock and the IMSA Street Stock classes provide an excellent outlet. Except for mandatory driver safety equipment, the Camaros that run in these series are virtually identical to those on dealer showroom floors.

During the 1980s, Camaros were the dominant machine in both sanctioning bodies, and more of the same is expected for this decade.

There were 111 SCCA Showroom Stock "ILE" models built in 1989, followed by sixty-two more in 1990. These race Camaros car-

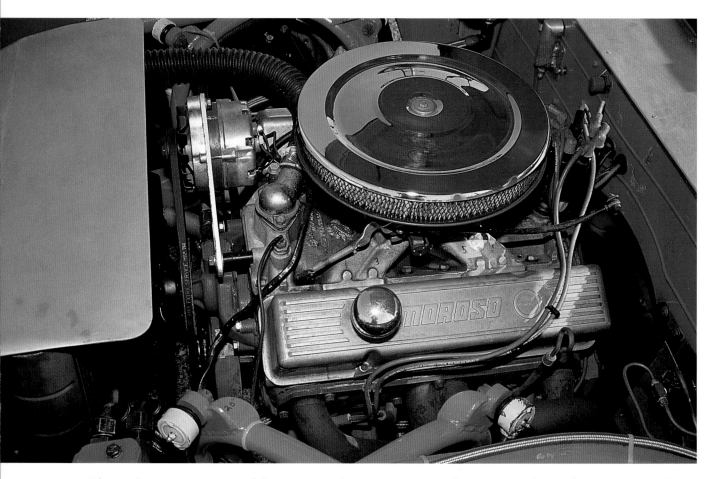

The engine compartment of the Foyt racer kept the factory connection with this small block powerplant. Daytonian Dale Gessaman is the owner of this historic machine.

ried aluminum drive shafts, Corvette-style front disc brakes, heavy-duty suspension, and fuel tank baffles.

Drag Racing

Bill "Grumpy" Jenkins first put Camaro in the national spotlight winning the SS/C NHRA national title with a win at the US Nationals in 1967. That victory established the 396 powerplant as a legitimate contender every time it hit the track. Jenkins was joined in the winners circle by Ben Wenzel who won Stock Eliminator with a B/Stock Z/28 Camaro powered by a 302ci small block.

Some of the more interesting Camaro drag cars were the outrageous early model machines produced by Dickie Harrell. Owning a performance shop in Kansas City, Harrell modified 427ci Camaros into "the new Super Camaro" configuration which pumped

The Canadian Players Series uses nearly stock Camaros for oval track competition.

out some 500 horses through the pipes. Very few of these cars have been located, but those that have are some of the most interesting and valuable of the muscle Camaro breed.

Jenkins dominated again in 1970 in the new Pro Stock class. With a '68 Rally Sport powered by a big block, Jenkins demonstrated quarter mile capabilities in the high nines at over 138mph.

In 1980, David Reher, Buddy Morris, and Lee Shepherd dominated Pro Stock with their second generation Z28 by winning six of ten events. Shepherd then scored a half dozen wins in 1981 and claimed the title.

Shepherd continued his Pro Stock title domination the following year with a 500ci "Rat" engine. Then he went on to score two more titles in 1983 and 1984. Bruce Allen continued Camaro's winning tradition winning eight NHRA and IHRA events in 1985, setting a Pro Stock speed record at over 192mph. He also clinched a third straight IHRA championship for the Reher-Morrison team.

From 1974 through 1989, a number of identically prepared Camaros were competed by drivers from different types of racing. This particular photo shows the competitors for that final IROC season. *Chevrolet Photo*

One of the most famous drag racing Camaros is this Dave Strickler Super Stock "F" Race Car. The car won the 1968 Super Stock World Championship title in Tulsa, Oklahoma on October 20, 1968.

In the more modern era, the Reher-Morrison Camaro was one of the top performers in NHRA Pro Stock competition. *Chevrolet Photo*

Index

Costume in Context

The Eighteenth Century

Jennifer Ruby

B.T. Batsford Ltd, London

Foreword

When studying costume it is important to understand the difference between fashion and costume. Fashion tends to predict the future – that is, what people *will* be wearing – and very fashionable clothes are usually worn only by people wealthy enough to afford them. For example, even today, the clothes that appear in fashionable magazines are not the same as those being worn by the majority of people in the street. Costume, on the other hand, represents what people are actually wearing at a given time, which may be quite different from what is termed 'fashionable' for their day.

Each book in this series is built round a fictitious family. By following the various members, sometimes over several generations – and the people with whom they come into contact – you will be able to see the major fashion developments of the period and compare the clothing and lifestyles of people from all walks of life. You will meet servants, soldiers, street-sellers and beggars as well as the very wealthy, and you will see how their different clothing reflects their particular occupations and circumstances.

Major social changes are mentioned in each period and you will see how clothing is adapted as people's needs and attitudes change. The date list will help you to understand more fully how historical events affect the clothes that people wear.

Many of the drawings in these books have been taken from contemporary paintings. During the course of your work perhaps you could visit some museums and art galleries yourself in order to learn more about the costumes of the period you are studying from the artists who painted at that time.

Acknowledgments

The sources for the drawings have, in many cases, been eighteenth-century paintings and prints. In particular, I would like to acknowledge the following:
frontispiece, after T. Hudson; page 16, after J. Van Aken; page 30, after H. Pickering; page 42, after J. Collet; page 47, after Moreau le Jeune; page 49, after D. Dighton; page 55, after Jean Baptiste Chardin; page 60, after J.A.D. Ingres; page 61, after H. Edridge. Colour plates: *At breakfast*, after Chardin; *In the country*, after Gainsborough; *Musicians*, after Tournières; *Children Playing*, after J. Singleton Copley; *Riding costume* after Joseph Wright.

Typeset by Tek-Art Ltd, Kent
and printed and bound in Great Britain
by The Bath Press, Bath
for the publishers
B.T. Batsford Ltd
4 Fitzhardinge Street
London W1H 0AH

ISBN 0 7134 5772 4

Contents

c. 1785

Date List

1700-1800	Enclosure Acts are passed throughout the century making things very difficult for the small farmer.
	For most of the century fashion takes its lead from France.
1714	George I comes to the throne. The Hanoverian court is very dull. The aristocracy lead the fashion rather than the King. Stiff formal clothes are fashionable: three piece suits and full-bottomed wigs for men. The bell shaped hoop petticoat is popular with women. The loose sack dress is often worn for informal occasions.
1721	The government imposes a ban on imported Indian printed and embroidered cottons and silks.
1727	The accession of George II.
1733	John Kay patents his fly-shuttle, which increases the speed of weaving.
1740s	Men are beginning to show a liking for comfortable country clothes for informal wear. The frock coat is seen more often. Women's skirts become very wide.
1749	Ban on imported metal embroidery, gold and silver lace.
1760s	The Macaroni Club is formed. The Macaroni fashions are very colourful and flamboyant.
	The sack dress has now become more fitted and is worn on formal occasions.
1760	Accession of George III.
1761	The Bridgewater Canal opens.
1764	Hargreaves invents the spinning jenny.
1766	Ban on imported French silks.
1769	The first steam engine.
1770s	The first fashion plates.
	The polonaise dress is very popular. Men are wearing the frock coat more and more. The cut is much narrower than previously.
1771	Richard Arkwright builds his first water powered spinning mill.
1772	Slavery becomes illegal in England.
1775	The War of American Independence.
1777	The Grand Trunk Canal opens.
1779	Samuel Crompton patents his 'mule' — a new type of spinning machine.
1780s	Children's clothes suddenly become less formal. Children are now dressed more comfortably and not as miniature adults.
1789	The French Revolution with its cries of 'Freedom and Liberty'.
1790s	Fashions do a turnabout. Stiffly formal styles, wigs and corsets are abandoned in favour of simplicity.

Introduction

The eighteenth century was a time of revolution and change. New ideas, inventions and philosophies accelerated progress and the old traditions were gradually eroded. The Agricultural and Industrial Revolutions and increased trade overseas meant better goods and services, which were brought to the public via an improved transport system. People were better informed because of the increased number of circulating books, newspapers and periodicals, and this lead to a greater awareness and questioning of the old ways. Music, art and literature added to the growing sophistication of society. The work of composers like Bach, Mozart and Handel, artists such as Gainsborough and Reynolds, and authors like Dr Johnson contributed towards more civilized living. It was an age of elegance and nowhere was this reflected more than in the changing styles of dress.

For most of the century, English fashion was dominated by French taste and styles which mirrored the luxury and dignity of the French aristocracy. The basic items in a man's wardrobe were his coat, waistcoat and breeches, which together formed his suit. A woman usually wore an open or closed robe supported by a hoop petticoat or panniers, which gave the gown the fashionable shape of the moment. Expensive wigs, lace and luxurious silks, satins and brocades gave the impression of wealth and elegance. False calves, false hair, false hips, false bosoms and false eyebrows were all worn during the period and, as skirts became wider and hairstyles became higher, it was as if the aristocracy were, by distorting and exaggerating their figures, parading their status and power with their clothing.

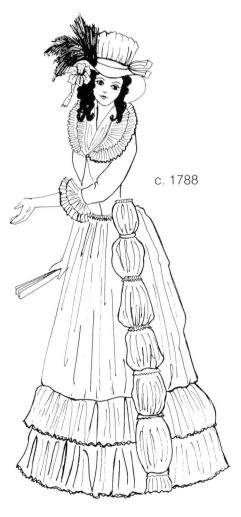

c. 1788

In contrast to this, the English did have a liking for simpler clothes for informal occasions. When relaxing in the country, men would often wear a frock coat. This garment had previously been worn only by common folk but was adopted by the wealthy for relaxing. It was simpler in cut and material than the fashionable coat and was gradually worn more and more until, by the 1780s, it had replaced the coat in popularity. Women often wore wrapping gowns or nightgowns when at home, though they were still rigidly corsetted and wore hoop petticoats beneath.

The final collapse of the rigid styles of fashionable dress was accelerated by the French Revolution which, like all major social upheavals, had a great effect on fashion. The cry was for freedom and liberty and, as the old aristocratic rule was swept away, so too were the established ways of dressing. Suddenly, powdered wigs, embroidered coats, brocaded gowns and fantastic hairstyles were all abandoned in favour of more simple styles. Men adopted plain coats and short hairstyles and women wore light muslin gowns and arranged their hair in soft curls, often tied around with a scarf in the ancient Greek fashion. It was as if fashion had done a turnabout by taking its lead from the country and creating a look which implied freedom and simplicity. This was a whole new way of looking at things and for the first time the dress

suit, c. 1768

frock coat,
c. 1768

court dress,
c. 1778

6

of country people was adapted for the wealthy and fashionable rather than the other way around.

It is interesting that children's clothes had undergone a similar revolution 20 years previously. Prior to the 1780s, children had always been dressed as miniature adults. However, at this time, due to the enlightened thinking of some philosophers, children's clothes became simpler and more practical, with little boys wearing plain coats and trousers (a garment previously reserved for sailors and country folk), and little girls wearing light muslin dresses.

Communications improved throughout the century. The new canal network and better roads meant that goods could be transported more easily to a public eager to pay for them. Travel increased both at home and abroad and this, coupled with the increased availability of newspapers and periodicals, meant that fashions could be seen and copied more quickly than previously. The fashion plate appeared in the 1770s and this also generated interest in the latest styles.

But fashion was not the concern of the poorer people, who were often the victims of all this progress. The Agricultural and Industrial Revolutions meant a change in the traditions of centuries. Many tenant farmers lost their land during the enclosure acts and many cottage workers found it impossible to compete with the new machinery of the Industrial Revolution. This meant that hundreds of poor flocked to the towns seeking work in the new factories. Many of them found jobs but worked for long hours in dreadful conditions and lived in factory houses which were no better than slums. Their clothing therefore was far from fashionable and amounted to whatever they could afford, which was usually plain clothes of linen and wool.

In between the two extremes of aristocracy and poor were the middle classes. These included professional people like doctors and lawyers, the great merchants and manufacturers who made their fortunes in industry, and the gentry. As money was not usually lacking with this group of people, their clothes generally depended upon their contact with fashionable circles. Merchants and manufacturers would obviously be in touch with the latest fashions and have the money to buy them. However, a country squire and his family living a long way from London would be a little behind with their fashions simply because they would not be moving in fashionable circles.

This book begins in 1714, as this date marks the end of the Stuart era and the beginning of Hanoverian rule. In it you will be able to follow an eighteenth-century family through several generations, looking at their changing dress. You will also meet other characters from all walks of life whose clothes and lifestyles you can contrast and compare. Try to think about some of the points above as you are reading and notice how clothes reflect people's background and circumstances. This will help you to understand what it was like to live in Georgian England.

c. 1792

A Duke, c. 1720

This gentleman is a Duke who owns a country estate in Bedfordshire. He is a Member of Parliament, so he also owns a large house in London in which he lives with his family when Parliament is in session.

He is wearing a velvet coat which is fitted to the waist and has side pleats from the hips. Under this he has on an embroidered satin waistcoat, a shirt with frilled cuffs, black velvet breeches and stockings. His stockings are called 'rolling stockings' because they are rolled down at the tops over garters. The Duke also wears a cravat and he is carrying his gloves and three-cornered hat, which is called a tricorne.

At this time it was the fashion for men to shave their heads and wear wigs. There were many different styles of wig which could be made from human hair (the most expensive), horse hair, goat hair or feathers. Wigs were usually powdered white or grey for dress occasions. By law this powder had to contain starch. When a gentleman had his wig powdered he would sit in a chair wearing a powdering jacket with his face and eyes protected by a paper mask or a funnel-shaped 'nosebag'. The hair would then be heavily greased and the barber would use bellows to apply the powder! Sometimes these elaborate styles would be left for many weeks before they were redone, so all kinds of small creatures frequently made their homes in fashionable wigs! The one pictured here is called a full-bottomed wig. Sometimes the Duke might wear a campaign wig when travelling. This was a three-tailed wig with a lock of hair tuned up at the end and tied in a knot.

Other items from the Duke's wardrobe are shown on the opposite page. His accessories would also include snuff boxes, canes, mittens, muffs, scarves and jewellery.

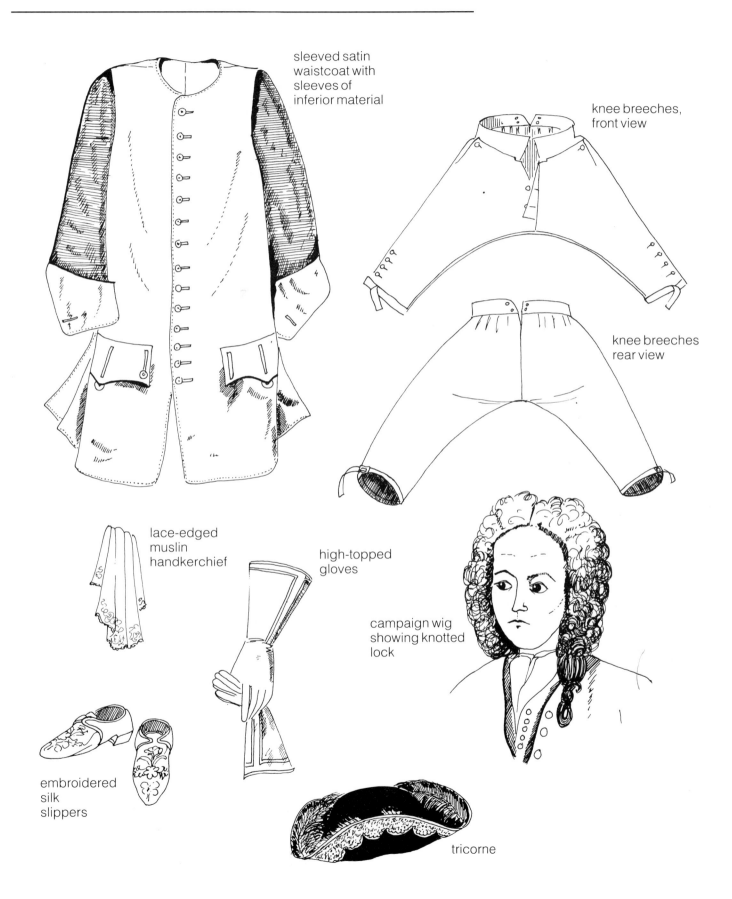

sleeved satin
waistcoat with
sleeves of
inferior material

knee breeches,
front view

knee breeches
rear view

lace-edged
muslin
handkerchief

high-topped
gloves

campaign wig
showing knotted
lock

embroidered
silk
slippers

tricorne

A Duchess, c. 1720

Here is the Duke's wife. She is wearing a fashionable sack dress which you can see from both the front and rear. It is a loose dress with draped cuffs and bow trims. The opening at the front is filled in with a stomacher. On her head, the Duchess is wearing a cap called a pinner, which has lappets (hanging pieces) attached at the sides. Her hair is tightly curled in this picture, although she sometimes wears it simply swept back into a bun on the top of her head.

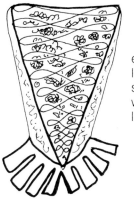

embroidered linen stomacher with cord lacing

Although this dress is very loose, the Duchess is tightly corsetted underneath. She is wearing a corset like the one pictured here and also a hoop petticoat which gives the dress its bell shape. This petticoat was very popular in the eighteenth century and was similar in shape to the farthingale which was worn in Tudor times.

The Duchess is very fond of make-up and uses red paint on her cheeks and lips. Like many women, she shaves her eyebrows off and replaces them with strips of mouseskin. She also wears face patches of different shapes and sizes which are made of black velvet or silk. At night she wears a band around her forehead covered with cream as this is thought to remove wrinkles.

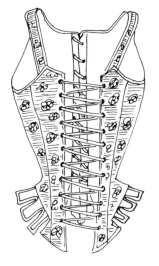

brocade open corset with front and back lacing

You can also see a few other items from her wardrobe pictured here.

silk petticoat with whalebone hoops

shoe in silk damask with wooden heel

leather clog stitched with white silk

embroidered slipper

drawstring purse

lace handkerchief

The Duke's Children, c. 1720

Here are the Duke's three children, Edward, Henrietta and baby Charles. At this time, it was the custom to dress little boys as girls until they were four or five years old, so all three children are wearing dresses.

Baby Charles is wearing a round-necked frock with a close-fitting bodice, a full skirt and turn-back cuffs. He has an apron over his dress and you can see his shirt frills at his neck and wrists. He is wearing a soft linen cap edged with lace and underneath this he has on a plain close-fitting cap. Babies wore caps night and day in the eighteenth century. Why do you think these were considered to be so important?

Edward is four years old. He is wearing a printed silk gown comprised of a separate bodice and skirt. The bodice is boned and is fastened at the back like the one pictured opposite. His frock has leading strings attached. These are rather like the reins that we use for very little children today.

Henrietta is five. She is wearing an embroidered silk gown with turn-back cuffs. This gown also has a separate bodice and skirt. The bodice is boned and fastens at the back and the low neckline is filled in with a tucker, which is a yoke of embroidered lace. Although she is very young, Henrietta is wearing a corset stiffened with whalebone under her dress and a hoop petticoat like the one pictured on page 11. Her shoes are made of linen and are beautifully embroidered.

Do you think it would be harmful for children to wear corsets and such restricting clothes? Consider some of the differences in the clothes worn by these children and those worn by very young children today.

child's corset
stitched linen
and whalebone

boy's wool bodice,
boned

embroidered
linen shoes

Afternoon Tea, c. 1722

In the eighteenth century it became very fashionable to drink tea. Here are the Duke and Duchess taking their afternoon tea, which is being served by Margaret, a parlourmaid.

The Duke is wearing a shorter full-bottomed wig, a velvet coat and waistcoat and breeches of silver damask. The Duchess is wearing a mob cap with hanging lappets and a satin wrapping gown which has a cross-over front and loose, turned-up cuffs. She is holding the only key to the black box at her feet which contains her tea caddies. Tea is very expensive so it is always locked away to prevent the servants from stealing it!

Margaret is wearing a pinner with the lappets pinned up in folds, a silk dress over a hoop petticoat and a smart white apron. You will notice that she is quite fashionably dressed. This is because she comes from a good family and has a fairly responsible position in the household.

At this time it was fashionable for wealthy families to have black page boys. These children were usually slaves who had been brought to England. Once in this country they remained in bondage and if they tried to escape they were recaptured and often punished. They were given gaudy and exotic clothes by their employers and usually wore a silver collar on which was engraved their master's name and address.

John, the Duke's little page, is wearing a turban with a feather, a scarlet coat with silver buttons and shoulder knot, a white shirt and white breeches and stockings. You can see his silver collar around his neck.

Slavery became illegal in England in 1772, when many unfortunate servants like John became free men.

A Farmer and his Family, c. 1730

Margaret's father William is a leasehold farmer on the Duke's estate. He is quite prosperous as he farms 300 acres and is able to sell his crops each year after the harvest. At present things are not too good for William because there has been a very good harvest everywhere, which means that the price of corn is low and he is making less money than usual.

Here is William sitting down to a meal with his wife Mary, his daughter Abigail, his son Charles and his daughter-in-law Rachel.

Rachel is seated on the left and is wearing a pinner with a ribbon on her head and a long handkerchief around her neck. This is not a pocket handkerchief as we know it today, but a large square of linen which Rachel has draped around her neck and threaded through the lacings on her bodice. Her gown has a fitted bodice and turned-back cuffs. The skirt of the gown has an open front and has been hitched up at the back revealing her brown woollen petticoat beneath. Over this she is wearing a white apron.

Her husband Charles is wearing a plain brown woollen coat, a white linen cravat and leather breeches. He is not wearing a wig because this would be inconvenient when he is working.

Abigail is wearing a mob cap with lappets tied under her chin and a woollen dress with a fitted bodice and flared skirt. Her mother is wearing a mob cap with lappets, a short handkerchief around her neck and a plain gown.

William is wearing a wig, a linen cravat, a woollen coat and waistcoat, breeches, stockings and stout shoes. He is following the custom of keeping his hat on indoors, but has temporarily removed it to say grace.

All the clothes shown here are very plain compared to those of the Duke and his family. There are no lace trimmings, fancy buttons or hoop petticoats. However, these garments are much more practical for working people.

The women of the house work very hard sewing, spinning, knitting and making butter, cheeses and preserves. On the right you can see Abigail, who is on her way to the local market to sell some cheese. She is wearing a mob cap, a floral print cotton gown and a white handkerchief and apron. She is also wearing a red cloak. This was an item of clothing that was popular with all country women in the eighteenth century. The hooded variety was usually called a riding cloak. Perhaps this was the garment that Little Red Riding Hood wore in the fairytale!

Abigail is wearing pattens on her feet. These are overshoes made with wooden soles raised on iron rings. She wears them to lift her out of the mud.

a patten

17

While Abigail is at the market, Mary is busy supervising the making of more cheese in the dairy. She is on the left of the picture and is wearing a mob cap with the lappets tied under her chin, a handkerchief around her neck, a plain woollen gown and a linen apron. She is talking to Martha who works for her. Martha's linen bodice has a deep basque which makes it look rather like a jacket; she has rolled up her bodice sleeves while she is at work. Her skirt is made of wool and is old and worn. On her head she is wearing a round-eared cap with the lappets pinned up and she has a piece of old sacking protecting her apron.

Rachel is wearing a similar hat to Martha; underneath it her hair is drawn up into a bun on top of her head. Her gown is made of printed calico and it has a striped pattern, which is unusual. The bodice laces down the back and has full three-quarter-length sleeves, which are gathered into a small cuff. Her shoes are made of linen.

Rachel is taking a piece of newly matured cheese to her father who has just returned from working outside and is feeling hungry.

What is Martha doing? Can you find out more about making cheese in the eighteenth century?

A Farm Labourer and his Family, c. 1732

This is Martha's husband Robin, who is a labourer on William's farm. Robin used to own a few strips of land himself which he farmed but an enclosure act forced him to surrender these. After the land was redistributed Robin was told that he would have to enclose his plot by putting a hedge around it. The cost of this would have been £30. This was more money than Robin had ever had so he was compelled to sell his land to William and become a labourer.

He is wearing a felt hat, a waistcoat of calamanco over a linen shirt, woollen breeches which are tied at the knee, stockings and leather shoes. He has tied his linen cravat around his waist as he is becoming hot doing his work.

Martha is spinning outside their cottage, which helps to earn a little extra money for the family. She is wearing a bedgown over her woollen dress. The bedgown was popular with working women for the whole of the eighteenth century. It was a short loose gown with a wrap-over front, which was often held in place by an apron tied over it. Martha's is made of linen and she has a piece of white linen tied around her head like a cap.

Their little son Ben is three years old. He is wearing a linen dress and a white apron. He has no cap or shoes and is eating a piece of dry bread. Compare his clothes with those of the Duke's children. Who do you think is the most comfortable?

Many women like Martha used to spin and weave at home. See if you can find out how things changed for them with the new inventions in the textile industry; for example, the flying shuttle and the spinning jenny.

Smugglers, c. 1734

This is Robin's brother Richard. He has found a more profitable and more dangerous way to earn a living than being a farm labourer. With the enclosure acts making things so difficult for small farmers, Richard decided that he would try his luck as a sailor. He has now become involved with a band of smugglers operating along the south coast of England. Here they are unloading brandy which has been brought illegally to England from France.

Richard has let his hair grow long and has it tied in a pigtail at the back. He is wearing a woollen cap, a plain linen shirt and very baggy breeches which are tucked into his thigh boots. These breeches were called slops and were worn by sailors for many years. (In 1756 the Navy Board set up a department to deal with clothing and it was known as the Slop Office!)

Richard's friend Harry is wearing a three-cornered hat, a scarf around his neck, a short coat, a striped waistcoat and trousers. Trousers were not usually worn in the eighteenth century and their use was restricted to labourers, sailors and soldiers. The majority of men did not start wearing them until the early nineteenth century.

Although the punishments were severe, smuggling was a widespread business in the eighteenth century. This was partly because many people did not see that there was anything wrong in it. Many fine ladies and gentlemen would even drive in their carriages to meet smugglers like Richard and Harry when they knew that a consignment of brandy, lace or tea had been landed. See if you can find out more about smugglers and the kind of lives they led.

A Wedding, c. 1744

It is now 1744 and we will return to the Duke and his family. This is Anne, the Duke's youngest daughter, who is 19. It is her wedding day and she is going to marry a young physician.

oblong hoop made of linen and cane (top view)

linen paniers

Anne is wearing a dress made of cream silk which has been embroidered in multi-coloured silks and silver thread and has matching shoes. The bodice has an open front and has been filled in with an embroidered stomacher. Underneath her gown she is wearing an oblong hoop like the one shown in the picture. The hoop is very wide from side to side and flat at the front and back. It is this that gives her gown the appearance of a hobby-horse parading sideways! (The same effect was also achieved when women wore paniers or 'false hips', also pictured opposite.)

She has her hair in curls at the back of her head and is wearing a simple lace cap with lappets and decorated with pearls. She is carrying her silk gloves.

Anne's dress is five feet wide! Many ladies were beginning to adopt this strange and ostentatious fashion and this often caused problems. A writer at the time observed:

> *"I have been in a moderate large room where there had been but two ladies who had not space to move without lifting up their petticoats higher than their grandmothers would have thought decent."*
> (*Universal Spectator – January 1741*)

Some women even became wedged in doorways!

Dr Andrew, the bridegroom, is pictured on the right. He is wearing a short powdered wig and a stock. This is a piece of fine linen which he is wearing in a band around his throat. It fastens at the back and leaves the ruffled edge of his shirt front visible at the front. He is also wearing a velvet coat lined with white satin, a white waistcoat with silver buttons from the neck to the hem, velvet breeches, white silk stockings and leather shoes with silver buckles.

After their marriage Andrew and Anne will live in a large house in London.

Two Wedding Guests, c. 1744

Here is Harriet, Anne's eldest sister. She has been married for some time and lives with her husband and children in London.

Harriet is wearing a satin sack dress for the wedding. It is more fitted than the earlier style of sack dress and has long embroidered robings. (Robings were the edges of a bodice and open skirt. Sometimes they reached only to the waist.) The open front of the bodice has been filled in with an embroidered stomacher.

Under her gown Harriet is wearing a fan hoop. This is like a hoop petticoat but is flatter in the front and back. It is very pliable, so Harriet can double it forward into two folds in order to pass through narrow spaces. Unfortunately, because the hoop is so pliable, it is liable to lift or turn inside out if caught by a wind, which could be very embarrassing! Can you imagine some of the problems that might arise at the wedding feast with many of the ladies having such wide skirts?

Harriet has her hair in curls and decorated with pearls and velvet ribbon.

This is James, Harriet's husband. He is wearing a velvet coat lined with silk. His waistcoat is made of white silk and is embroidered with gold thread. It has vertical pocket flaps which are unusual. He is wearing his sword belt over his waistcoat, which is also uncommon.

Like Andrew, James is wearing a stock, velvet breeches and white stockings. His wig is a small one with the front and sides curled and the hanging ends tied at the back with a taffeta bow into a tail or 'queue'. He has high-topped gloves and is carrying a hat and a cane with a carved head.

Another guest standing near James has a similar wig which you can see from the rear. Sometimes the tail of a wig was placed in a black bag matching the ribbon. This was then known as a 'bag wig'.

See if you can draw a picture of some of the other wedding guests. Make their clothes very elaborate with beautiful embroidery and lace trimmings.

A London Doctor, c. 1755

We will now move forward to the year 1755 and to Andrew and Anne's home in London. Here is Doctor Andrew in his study. He is wearing a physical wig. This was a wig commonly worn by members of the learned professions, particularly doctors, and was either frizzed or arranged in horizontal curls like the one pictured here.

The doctor is also wearing a matching satin coat and breeches. The coat has button loop fastenings, a small standing collar and open cuffs. His breeches are left open to expose the knees as this is fashionable. His stockings are made of silk and the buckles on his shoes are silver.

When the doctor is relaxing he often wears a banyan. This is like a dressing gown which crosses over and fastens with a clasp. Here he is wearing a bright red satin banyan with a yellow lining. Underneath this he has on a short waistcoat and breeches unbuttoned at the knee. He has three buttons on his waistcoat undone because it is fashionable to stand with a hand tucked inside the waistcoat. He is wearing a velvet turban over his shaved head and heel-less and backless slippers (mules) on his feet.

You will notice the doctor's lace cuffs in both pictures. Lace was very costly and throughout the century an abundance of lace was used as a display of wealth. Lace dangling over the wearer's hands would signify that he did not get his hands dirty and was above any kind of menial work. Lace was frequently smuggled into England and wealthy men and women saw nothing wrong in obtaining their finery from the little bands of smugglers like Richard and Harry who operated up and down the country.

The doctor's accessories include snuff boxes, watches, walking sticks, gloves, handkerchiefs and tooth-pick cases made of tortoiseshell.

The Doctor's Wife, c. 1755

Here is Anne at her London home. As the wife of a wealthy physician, she can afford to wear beautiful and expensive clothes.

Here she has on a straw 'milkmaid' hat, which is trimmed with ribbon. It is held in place by a ribbon at the back of her neck and is worn over a small white linen cap. The sack is now becoming a more formal dress, and Anne's has a tight bodice with wide robings and box pleats at the back which hang from the shoulders (as in the diagram opposite). Her sleeves are tight to the elbow and have a treble flounce. The dress is made of silk and is beautifully embroidered. She has a lace-edged handkerchief crossed over her chest and fastened with a bow and she is putting on her white silk gloves.

In the picture on the far right Anne is wearing a round-eared cap and a tippet. This is a shoulder cape, in the front of which she has placed a bosom bottle containing water to keep her flowers fresh. It was common practice for women to wear flowers in this way as it helped to counteract unpleasant odours!

The fashionable look is for a white skin tinged with red, so Anne puts white powder on to her face and uses rouge. She also likes to wear velvet face patches.

See if you can find out more about cosmetics in the eighteenth century. In particular, the harmful effects of some of the face powders, which often contained lead and mercury. Many women had disfigured complexions because of the prevalence of diseases such as smallpox. Velvet patches therefore were often useful to disguise pockmarks on the skin. Tooth decay and loss were also very common, so ladies would wear plumpers (small cork balls) inside their cheeks to fill out the hollows caused by lost teeth. False teeth were sometimes hooked on to conceal discoloured front teeth. These teeth were human and were often purchased from poor people who needed a little extra money! Perhaps you would like to compare this with our standards of hygiene today.

Also pictured here are two other items from her wardrobe. The pockets are worn under her dress and over her petticoat. Can you imagine how inconvenient this would be?

white linen pockets embroidered coloured silks

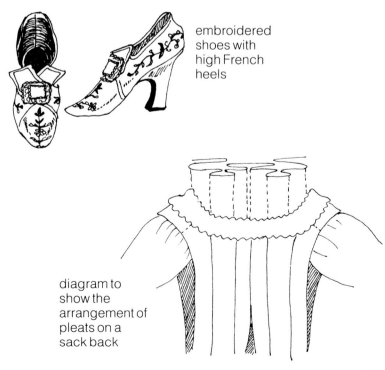

embroidered shoes with high French heels

diagram to show the arrangement of pleats on a sack back

The Doctor's Children, c. 1755

Here is Anne with her two youngest children; Caroline, who is three years old, and baby Henry. Anne is wearing a satin dress with short robings. Her stomacher is trimmed with a ladder of bows decreasing in size from above. These are called échelles. Her soft linen cap does not have lappets and is trimmed with lace.

Caroline is also wearing a round-eared cap. Her dress is made of satin and has a tight bodice, fastening at the back, and a separate skirt. Even though she is so young, Caroline is wearing stays to give her the correct fashionable shape and also a hoop petticoat.

The baby is wearing a white silk dress and a fine muslin apron trimmed with lace.

Musicians, c. 1715-20

In the country, c. 1748

At breakfast, c. 1750

Rich and poor, children, c. 1770

Riding costume, c. 1769

Polanaise, c. 1770-1780

Children playing, c. 1784

Ladies' fashions, c. 1788-90

A Brother and Sister, c. 1755

Here are the doctor's eldest children, Eleanor, aged ten, and nine-year-old Giles. They have been out playing in the garden. Eleanor is wearing a round-eared cap and a similar dress to Caroline's with a tight bodice and flared skirt supported by a hoop petticoat. Giles is wearing a velvet coat with turn-back cuffs, velvet breeches, a single-breasted silk waistcoat, a fine linen shirt and a neck ribbon. He is not wearing a wig.

Once again, these children are dressed in clothes which seem to us to be very restricting. Eighteenth-century children did find their clothes uncomfortable. One lady, recalling her childhood in the 1780s, wrote that the first time she wore her stays she felt as though she were in purgatory because they were so tight around her chest.*

* (*Elizabeth Ham* by Herself, 1783-1820)

Three Servants, c. 1755

Dr Andrew is very wealthy and he has a large number of servants. Here you can see three of them.

Jane is one of the housemaids. She is wearing a mob cap, a jacket-like linen bodice, a plain linen skirt, an apron and a neckerchief. Jane spends most of her day cleaning. It is hard work but she does not mind as her employers are kind and she has many friends among the other servants.

Ralph is a running footman. This means that his job is to run in front of his master's coach. His clothing needs to be both light in weight and colour so that he can be easily seen when the coach is travelling after dark. He is dressed in a white shirt and petticoat breeches. These are very wide breeches that resemble a divided skirt. They were, in fact, fashionable in the 1660s but running footmen still wear them a hundred years later as they are very convenient for running in when the current fashion is for tight breeches. For decency's sake, Ralph's breeches are weighted down by a heavy fringe. This is necessary as he often does not wear any drawers underneath! He is also wearing a blue silk sash, a cap with a tassel, and he is carrying a stave with a silver ball on the head. The ball unscrews and is a small container in which he keeps a little wine to drink when he is thirsty! Ralph is extremely fit as he runs many miles every day.

Ralph's brother John is also a servant in the Doctor's house. He has quite a good position so he dresses in clothes that are of good quality, though a little old fashioned. He is wearing a wig with a queue, a linen neckcloth, breeches, a waistcoat and a coat which is more flared than is currently fashionable. His stockings are cotton and his shoes are made of leather.

Milkmaids on May Day, c. 1755

We will now go outside into the streets of London. It is May Day and many people are enjoying the celebrations. This is Ellen, one of Jane's sisters, who is a milkmaid. She is dancing with two of her friends, Hannah and Beth.

All three girls are wearing straw hats over their linen caps, cotton dresses with tight bodices and turned back cuffs and flared skirts. They are not wearing hoop petticoats, as these would hamper their movements too much whilst they are working. They all have white linen aprons and their hats and bodices are decorated with ribbons and flowers.

These milkmaid hats were very popular at this time with all classes of women. (You will remember that Anne was wearing one on page 30.) It is interesting that on this occasion a fashion evolved that originated from a garment worn by common people instead of the usual course of events, when fashion came from the rich and was later adopted by the poor.

Milkmaids were usually joined by chimney sweeps for these May Day celebrations. Draw a picture of the festivities and include milkmaids and chimney sweeps. *See* if you can find out what they might have had to eat and drink.

Street Vendors, c. 1755

The streets of London were very noisy in the eighteenth century and were alive with pedlars, hawkers and other wanderers who sold their wares to passers by.

This is Jane and Ellen's mother, who is selling bread and pastries that she has baked herself. She is wearing a straw hat over a mob cap, a short cape and a checked cotton apron over her dress. She also has on a double pocket over her apron in which she puts her money. Her dress is quite short so it does not get soiled from the dirt and filth on the street.

Just around a corner we meet a spoon seller and a tinker. The spoon seller is wearing a red skirt lined with cotton which she has pinned up revealing her linen petticoat beneath. Her bodice is simply her stays, which are worn over a cotton smock. Over all of this she has a cloak for extra warmth. She is wearing two aprons and the inevitable straw hat over a mob cap.

The tinker is wearing an old felt hat, a woollen coat and breeches, a bibbed leather apron, woollen stockings, and leather shoes. He has a pair of bellows strapped to his back and is banging an old tin pan.

See if you can find out more about street sellers, their lifestyles and the kind of clothes that they wore.

A Visit to the Theatre, c. 1766

It is now 1766. Here is Dr Andrew and his wife, both a little older now, who are dressed and ready for a trip to the theatre.

The doctor is wearing a suit of embossed and embroidered scarlet velvet. The coat and waistcoat have a noticeable front curve which results in a slimmer look, without the side pleats that were previously fashionable. He is also wearing a bag wig and a solitaire which is a black tie worn over his stock. His stockings are made of white silk and he has gold buckles on his shoes.

Anne is wearing an elaborately trimmed sack dress with a train. It is made of pink silk and has a tight-fitting bodice with robings. The skirt is open at the front, revealing a matching pink silk petticoat which is flounced and furbelowed. Her stomacher is also highly decorated with ruchings and échelles. Around her neck she is wearing a lace ruff and on her head a silk turban which complements her hair style, which is raised on pads.

This new style of hairdressing marks the beginning of a fashion for very tall and elaborate styles which came into vogue later in the century.

The couple look magnificent in all their finery. They are on their way to Covent Garden to see a play. Theatre, opera and music became very popular in the eighteenth century – but one of the disadvantages of theatre-going was the audience. A rather strange custom existed whereby privileged spectators were allowed to sit on the stage which meant the actors were crowded and the view was blocked for many others in the audience. In addition to this many people thought nothing of chatting or wandering around during a performance, which must have been very distracting. David Garrick, a very famous actor and theatre manager, tried to improve things with his strong management of the theatre in Drury Lane.

The doctor and his wife might also have gone to the opera or enjoyed music by Handel.

Hairdressing, c. 1770

Wigs were an important part of any gentleman's wardrobe in the eighteenth century. They needed constant attention, which gave regular work to barbers, who would dress them with pomatum (a scented ointment) to keep the curls in place and then powder them for their clients. The powder was pulverised rice starch, which was scented and applied with a large powder puff or blower.

Here is Dr Andrew, who is being visited by his hairdresser William Matisse, who is a Frenchman. William is wearing a bag wig, a tight, short coat which serves him both as a waistcoat and a coat, and breeches. William is applying powder to Dr Andrew's wig with a powder puff.

Dr Andrew is wearing a powdering gown to protect his clothes. The powder was often a problem because it got everywhere and made a fine mess of furniture, clothes and carpets.

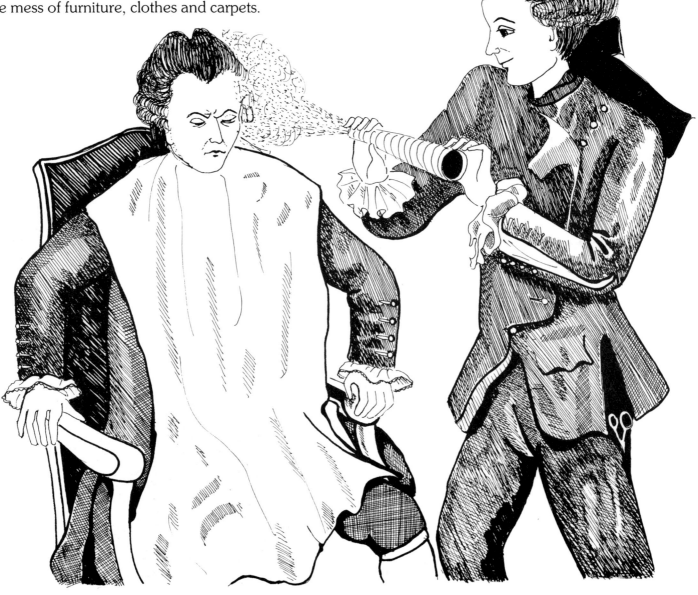

calash

Ladies' hairstyles were also very elaborate at this time, although they did not usually wear wigs. Instead, their own hair was used to create fancy styles to which puffs, rolls, wires, pads and sometimes false hair were added to give extra height. These styles would take hours to create and were very expensive. Consequently they would be left for weeks undisturbed, which was very unhygienic. They were also uncomfortable, as the wires and pads would frequently cause headaches. In Fanny Burney's novel *Evelina*, the heroine describes her new hairstyle as follows:

"I have just had my hair dressed. You can't think how oddly it feels; full of powder and black pins, and a great cushion on the top of it. I believe you would hardly know me, for my face looks quite different to what it did before my hair was dressed. When I shall be able to make use of a comb for myself I cannot tell, for my hair is so much entangled, 'frizzled' they call it, that I fear it will be very difficult." (1778)

Here is Anne in her chemise and stays at her mirror. Her hair has been dressed into a tall style by her hairdresser and she has put a muslin cap over it so that it is not disturbed when she is in bed. In fact, she will sleep in a half sitting position all night so that her hair is kept in place! When she goes out Anne sometimes wears a calash to protect her hairstyle. This is a large hood made of silk and supported by cane arches.

A Macaroni, c. 1772

Now we will see what has been happening to the doctor's children.

The Macaroni club was formed in the 1760s by a group of young men who had travelled in Italy and had brought back some new ideas in fashion. By the 1770s, however, the word Macaroni was used to describe young men who wore extremes of fashion such as towering wigs and tight suits. Henry is a Macaroni and he is wearing a bag wig of enormous height with large side curls. His coat is called a frock coat (distinguishable from the ordinary coat by its turned down collar). It is very tight fitting and has decorative buttons. Frock coats were now becoming very fashionable, although they were previously reserved for country wear or for relaxing. Henry is also wearing a short waistcoat with slit pockets, striped breeches, and he is carrying a small round hat under his arm. He has flat-heeled dancing pumps on his feet, and has tied a silk ribbon around his sword handle – which probably means that he has no intention of using his sword!

In order to achieve an unbroken line in their dress the Macaronis favoured an inside coat pocket in preference to the usual outside pocket with a flap. So it is to the Macaronis that gentlemen of today owe the inside breast pockets on their coats!

The Macaronis were often accused of looking somewhat effeminate. Henry certainly appears very different to his older brother Giles, who has joined the infantry.

A Soldier, c. 1775

Giles is wearing his uniform, which consists of a short red coat and waistcoat with gold trimming and silver buttons. His breeches are white and he has black half-gaiters buttoned over his ankles to protect his shoes and stockings from mud and grime. He wears a special leather cap encircled with chains and is carrying his gun. His powder horn is strapped around his shoulder and he is wearing a hatchet at his belt.

Giles will soon be going to America to fight against the Americans in the War of Independence. The English were very proud of their soldiers at this time and no-one believed that the American colonies would eventually win the struggle. George III believed that his fine forces would quickly bring the American 'ruffians' under control and the struggle would soon be over. However, things turned out very differently.

Perhaps you could think about what might have happened to Giles in the war. You could also find out more about the uniforms of the soldiers who fought on both sides.

People of Fashion, c. 1777

Eleanor, the doctor's eldest daughter, has now married a rich young landowner and MP called Frederick Woodford. Frederick is wearing a frock coat with flat decorative buttons and slit sleeves, a short waistcoat and leather shoes with low tongues and square buckles. His outfit is in fact very similar to Henry's. Compare the two and decide what the difference is between a Macaroni and an ordinary man of fashion.

Frederick is waiting for Eleanor, who is pictured on the right talking to her sister Caroline and her new husband Edmund. Both women are wearing polonaise dresses, which are the height of fashion.

The essential feature of the polonaise was the overskirt, which was bunched up into three puffs behind, completely uncovering the petticoat. This was achieved either by inside cords which could be pulled up and knotted, with buttons and loops, or with ribbon ties.

Here you can see the polonaise both from the front and rear. These dresses are very elaborate with their frills, flounces and bows and are complemented by the ladies' fancy hairstyles and trimmed and feathered hats.

Edmund is also a very rich young man. He has just inherited a cotton mill in the Midlands on the death of his father and he and Caroline are moving there to live.

A Mill Owner's Wife, c. 1785

It is now 1785 and Caroline and Edmund are living in the Midlands in a fine house with their servants and children.

In the far picture you can see Caroline wearing the latest fashions. Her hair is frizzled at the sides and she has a thick loop of hair hanging down her neck. Under her hat she is wearing a dormeuse, which is a lacey cap with a loose crown and side flaps called wings. Her gown is an open robe which is worn over a false rump. This is a pad stuffed with cork which fits at the back of her waist and is tied with tapes in the front. (These false rumps or 'bums' were extremely popular and reappeared in the nineteenth century, when they were called bustles.) Over her petticoat Caroline is wearing a fine silk gauze apron and on a hook beside her you can see her silk pelerine. This is a kind of cape with long front pendants which she often wears indoors.

mob cap

Hairstyles and hats are now very large and elaborate, as you can see from the pictures opposite. In the lower picture, Caroline is wearing her hair 'à la conseilleur', which means that she has long, loose tresses down her back. Pads, supports and false hair are necessary to achieve the fashionable look and for a special occasion she will add decorations of ribbons, feathers, flowers and jewels, giving the style great height.

Rouge is not so fashionable now but Caroline still wears patches upon her face and false eyebrows. Sometimes she might wear a false bosom. You can imagine that many women like Caroline must have looked quite different when they were undressed and had removed all their artificial aids to beauty!

The following quote comes from a journal of 1786. A lady is speaking to her maid:

> *"Lay my head on the top of the drawers; put my bottom on the chair and the hips above it. Take care of my bosom and don't ruffle it. Lay this eye on to my dressing-box; here take this shoulder, lay it by my head, and lock up my teeth in the cloth bag." (Ipswich Journal – 1786)*

large hat worn with sideways tilt — hair 'à la conseilleur'

Do you think women have as many artificial accessories today?

The Owner of a Cotton Mill, c. 1787

Here is Caroline's husband Edmund, who owns a large cotton mill. You can see from his outfit that men's clothes have not changed a great deal over the last ten years.

He is wearing a frock coat which is cut away at the front and has a high collar and small round cuffs. Waistcoats are now considerably shorter than the top coat and Edmund's is double breasted with small pearl buttons. He is wearing breeches and low shoes with large rectangular buckles. His hat is called a bicorne. Its brim is turned up high at the front and behind and it is trimmed with a small cockade.

Edmund is wearing a small toupee with side curls, which you can see more clearly on the opposite page. Also pictured are some other items from his wardrobe. When riding, he often wears spatterdashes, which are long gaiters. These protect his legs and ankles from the wet and mud. He has a large collection of waistcoats, breeches and shoes and many accessories, including breast buckles and brooches, enamelled toothpick cases, walking sticks, gloves, jewellery and umbrellas (which were introduced for men in 1756).

Many men at this time took almost as long over their dressing as women. Some wore rouge and perfume and false calves were popular. These were used to improve the shape of the legs and were made of parchment, pads or bandages.

Do you think that, on average, men and women take as much time over their appearance today?

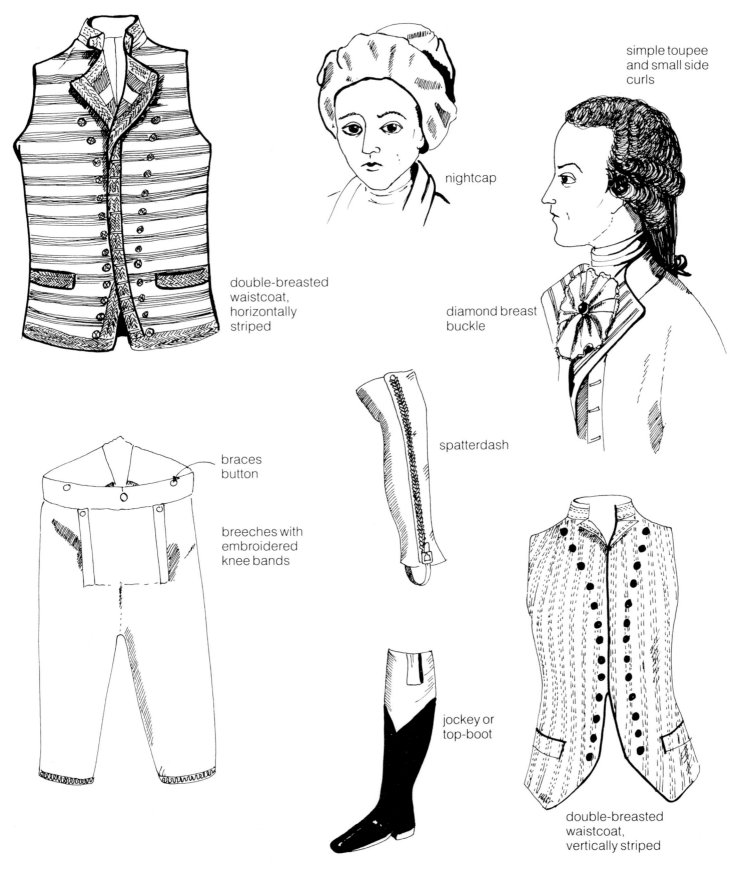

double-breasted waistcoat, horizontally striped

nightcap

simple toupee and small side curls

diamond breast buckle

braces button

breeches with embroidered knee bands

spatterdash

jockey or top-boot

double-breasted waistcoat, vertically striped

Children's Clothes, c. 1787

During the 1780s a revolution occured in children's dress. Prior to this time, little boys wore dresses until they were old enough to be breeched; then they were dressed as miniature adults. Little girls wore muslin dresses until they were four or five and then wore replicas of their mothers' clothes. In the 1780s, however, the fashions for children suddenly became more comfortable and practical. Instead of going directly from baby dresses into adult breeches, little boys were now dressed in trousers – a garment previously reserved for sailors and countrymen. They wore these with simple shirts and sometimes with the addition of a sash at the waist. Little girls began to wear the light muslin dresses of babyhood for longer, so that by the 1780s it was fashionable for teenage girls to be wearing high waisted gowns of soft material with coloured sashes, instead of the restricting corsetted gowns of fashionable women.

It is interesting that eventually trousers became fashionable for men and light muslin dresses became fashionable for women, so, for the first time in history, children were setting the trends for the future. (In fact, a girl born in 1780 would have worn the same style of dress until she was about 30, because the clothes of her childhood would have become fashionable when she became a woman!)

Caroline's children are playing in the garden. Stephen, who is six, is wearing cotton trousers with a shirt of soft white lawn and a linen coat with curved fronts and a narrow tail.

The two girls, Mary and Beatrice, are both wearing light cotton dresses with sashes, aprons and mob caps. Jonathan is still in his baby dress and cap. Apart from the large hats worn by Beatrice and Stephen, the children look quite comfortable, especially when their clothes are compared with those worn by their mother when she was a child (page 32).

A Mill Worker and his Family, c. 1788

This is Adam, who is employed in the mill workshops, making and repairing iron nails, bolts, brackets and different fittings which are needed to keep the mill machinery in working order. He lives with his wife and children in a small terraced house which he rents from the mill owner. Edmund had about 100 houses built for the mill workers and their families so that they could be near to their place of employment.

Adam is wearing a linen shirt and breeches, woollen stockings and leather shoes, and he has a leather apron tied around his waist.

His wife Hetty is at home doing the washing. She is wearing a mob cap, a bedgown which is held in place with an apron, a woollen skirt and wooden clogs. Hetty and Adam's youngest son Sam is blowing bubbles with the soap suds. His coat is very old fashioned compared to that worn by Stephen (page 52), it is rather old and used to belong to his elder brother. Sam is also wearing a linen shirt and breeches, woollen stockings and leather shoes.

Adam used to have his own small business making nails in a neighbouring village. However, when times became hard he answered an advertisement for mill workers that was pasted up in the village square. The job attracted him because of the regular wages and the house for a nominal rent. His eldest children work in the mill and this brings in a little extra money; so he is better off than before. However, Adam liked the freedom of having his own business and Hetty does not like living so close to the dirty, noisy mill.

The New Fashions, c. 1794

We will now move on to the year 1794 to have a look at the clothes of Beatrice and Mary, who are now fashionable young women.

The clothes of both men and women altered quite dramatically in the 1790s. The French Revolution, with its message of freedom, had a profound effect on fashion. Suddenly the stiff, embroidered, corsetted clothes and powdered wigs were swept away and replaced with a softer, simpler look. Women abandoned their bustles, false hair, corsets and the rich materials that their dresses had previously been made of. Instead, they wore high-waisted dresses of light material such as muslin or lawn. These were sometimes semi-transparent, so it was necessary to wear white or pink tights underneath. Because the dresses were so flimsy pockets became impractical, so ladies began to carry small bags called reticules with them everywhere they went. Hairstyles were also simplified and many women had their hair cut quite short. Heel-less slippers replaced the high-heeled shoes of the previous decade.

Beatrice and Mary are wearing comfortable house clothes of muslin. They both have pleated caps of white lawn trimmed with coloured ribbon and flounce-trimmed skirts. Beatrice (seated) is wearing a caraco which is a three-quarter length jacket. Together with her skirt, this is known as a caraco dress. Mary is wearing a long white coat which fastens only at the waist. Each girl is wearing a fichu ather neck and low-heeled slippers, like those pictured opposite.

Also on this page you can see Beatrice's hairstyle more clearly. It is very different from the previous styles of the century. In fact, it is similar to the styles worn in the 1920s! Beatrice and Mary usually wear small bonnets rather than large or fancy hats. Sometimes they wear turbans trimmed with feathers like the one opposite.

It is interesting that great social upheavals usually have a dramatic effect on fashion. You could compare the changes in dress after the French Revolution with the changes that occured in the 1920s following the First World War. In both cases, women abandoned their corsets, large hats and elaborate hairstyles in favour of a greater freedom. Can you think of any other similarities?

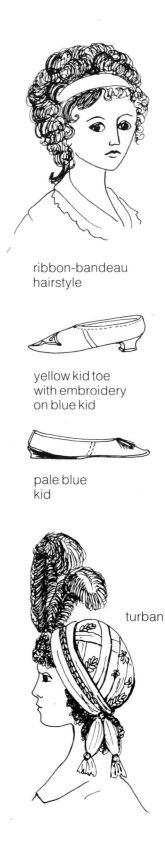

ribbon-bandeau hairstyle

yellow kid toe with embroidery on blue kid

pale blue kid

turban

pin-on flower spray for hair or hat – made of gold lace, metal thread, beads and feathers

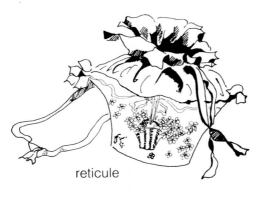

reticule

57

Male Fashion, c. 1795

Here is Stephen, Mary and Beatrice's brother, who is dressed in the latest fashions.

He is wearing a frock coat with lapels, a short double-breasted waistcoat and a muslin cravat which is wound around his neck three times and then tied in a bow at the front. Usually he wears breeches but today he is wearing pantaloons, which are close fitting tights shaped to his leg and ending at his ankles. His boots are called Hussar buskins and he is carrying his gloves and cane.

In this picture Stephen is wearing his own hair as wigs are no longer fashionable. In the picture on the right he has had his hair cut in the 'Brutus crop' style. In that same picture he is wearing two waistcoats. Although the under waistcoat is worn mainly for warmth, it is designed to be seen and the visible portion is made of bright silk material.

The fashion in men's hats has also altered and the three cornered hat, popular for nearly a century, is now being replaced by different styles of round hat like that pictured opposite. This is a primitive form of the top hat worn by men in the nineteenth century. The other two pictures show the frock coat from behind and one of Stephen's many waistcoats.

You might like to compare Stephen's outfit with that of his great grandfather, the Duke, who appeared at the beginning of the book (page 8). What are the main differences in their clothing?

rear view of coat

double-breasted waistcoat worn over under-waistcoat – cropped hair

double-breasted waistcoat of grey satin, woven with flower border

hat of light brown woollen cloth with brown silk band

Conclusion

We now come to the end of the eighteenth century and you can see how radically different clothes are now to what they were at the beginning. Corsets, wiring, wigs, supports and the heavily embroidered fabrics which symbolized wealth, status and the aristocracy have now given way to clothes which symbolize freedom and simplicity.

A classical look is now popular with women, and many ladies dress in styles that might have been worn in ancient Greece.

Here is Mary and her fiancé John. Mary is wearing a high-waisted dress of light cotton with sleeves of dimity (which is a cotton with a raised pattern). Her hair is bound around her head with a gauze scarf and she has a fringe of curls in the Grecian style. She wears flat-heeled pumps on her feet and a cashmere shawl around her shoulders.

c. 1800

As always, however, being fashionable is not always practical, as this style of dress is not really suited to the English climate! Some women even dampen the material of their gowns so that it clings to their bodies like the folds of the Greek dresses in antique statues. What problems do you think this might cause?

John is wearing his hair cut and curled in a short crop. His coat is double-breasted with long, tight sleeves and tails at the back. His breeches are tight and he has boot garters over his knees, which are straps attached to his boots so that the soft leather does not fall down as he walks. He is carrying his round hat, gloves and cane.

As we leave Mary and John looking forward to their marriage and to a new century, perhaps you would like to reflect on the changes that have taken place in styles of dress. The eighteenth century is often called the 'Age of Enlightenment'. Try and think about what this means and how it relates to fashionable clothing.

c. 1800

Glossary

à la conseilleur	A hairstyle in which the hair was worn in long tresses down the back *(page 48)*
bag wig	A wig with the back hair enclosed in a black silk bag. It was usually worn for dress occasions *(pages 40, 42, 44, 46)*
banyan	A man's dressing gown, often brightly coloured *(page 29)*
basque	A band of material attached to the bodice at the waistline *(page 18)*
bedgown	A lady's cross-over gown of three-quarter length. It was usually made of cotton and worn by working women *(pages 21, 55))*
bicorne	A man's hat which had the brim turned up high in front and behind, obscuring the crown *(page 50)*
brutus crop	A short hairstyle for men which came into fashion in the late eighteenth century *(page 59)*
calamanco	A worsted fabric *(page 20)*
calash	A lady's hood made of silk and supported by cane arches *(page 43)*
campaign wig	A three-tailed wig with two locks hanging over each shoulder *(page 9)*
caraco	A lady's three-quarter length jacket. When teamed with a matching skirt, this was known as caraco dress *(page 56)*
damask	Silk material with a raised pattern *(page 14)*
dimity	Cotton with a raised pattern – usually spots *(page 60)*
dormeuse	A woman's frilled indoor cap, similar to a mob cap *(page 49)*
échelles	A ladder of bows decreasing in size from above which decorated the stomacher *(pages 32, 41)*
fan hoop	Similar to a hoop petticoat but flatter in the front and back *(page 26)*
fichu	A woman's small triangular shawl, often made of lace *(page 56)*
furbelow	A horizontal flounce of material on a woman's petticoat *(page 41)*
handkerchief	A large square of muslin, gauze, linen or silk, folded around the neck *(pages 16, 30)*
hoop petticoat	A petticoat reinforced with cane hoops to give the skirt a fashionable bell shape, until the 1730s *(pages 11, 13, 32, 33)*. From 1730-1740 the skirt flattened at the front and back and became the fan hoop *(page 26)*. For court or special occasions ladies often wore oblong hoops or paniers, which were basket-like supports worn over the hips. These gave the skirt a very exaggerated shape *(page 24)*
hussar buskins	Long-toed short boots *(page 58)*
lappets	Long streamers attached to a woman's cap *(pages 10, 18)*
leading strings	Long bands of material attached to a child's frock at the back *(page 12)*
milkmaid hat	A straw hat with a wide brim and a low crown *(pages 30, 36, 37, 38, 39)*
mob cap	A woman's cap with a puffed-out crown, deep frilled border and side pieces *(pages 14, 16, 17, 34, 38, 39, 48, 53, 55)*
open robe	A dress with a gap in the front of the skirt in the shape of an inverted V, which allowed the petticoat to be seen beneath. (A closed robe consisted of a bodice and a petticoat with no opening in the front skirt.) *(pages 41, 49)*
pantaloons	Close-fitting men's tights shaped to the leg and ending at the ankles *(page 58)*
pelerine	A light cape with long front pendants which was often worn indoors *(page 49)*
pinner	A circular cap surrounded by a frill of linen and sometimes worn with lappets *(pages 10, 15)*
physical wig	A bob wig with all-over frizzled curls, which was usually worn by professional men *(page 28)*
plumpers	Small cork balls which were placed in the mouth to fill out hollow cheeks *(page 31)*
polonaise	A woman's gown, the overskirt of which would be bunched out into three puffed-out draperies behind, completely exposing the petticoat all round *(page 47)*
pomatum	A scented ointment used to dress the hair *(page 42)*
queue	A lock of hair tied or knotted at the back *(page 27)*
robings	The edges of a bodice or open skirt *(pages 26, 41)*
rolling stockings	Over-the-knee stockings, turned down over garters *(page 8)*
round-eared cap	A woman's cap shaped to curve around the face with a frilled border *(pages 32, 33, 36, 37)*
sack dress	At the beginning of the eighteenth century this was a loose, informal gown which later became more fitted and worn on formal occasions *(pages 11, 24, 26, 30)*
slops	Loose, baggy breeches worn by sailors *(page 22)*
solitaire	A black tie worn over a stock *(page 40)*

spatterdash	Long gaiters *(page 51)*
stock	A neck-cloth fastening at the back. It was usually made of plain or pleated linen *(pages 25, 27, 40)*
stomacher	A V-shaped panel used as a fill-in for an open bodice. It would usually be stiffened and embroidered *(pages 10, 24, 26, 32, 41)*
tippet	A small shoulder cape *(page 31)*
tricorne	A three-cornered hat *(pages 9, 20, 23, 40, 46, 47)*
tucker	A yoke of embroidered lace or fabric worn to fill in a low-cut bodice *(page 13)*
wrapping gown	A woman's gown with a wrap-over front, which was often secured with a belt *(page 14)*

Book List

Anderson-Black, J. & Garland, M.	*A history of fashion*, Orbis, 1975
Asser, Joyce	*Historic hairdressing*, Pitman, 1966
Barthorp, Michael	*British infantry uniforms since 1660*, Blandford Books, 1982
Bradfield, Nancy	*Costume in detail 1730-1930*, Harrap, 1968
Bradfield, Nancy	*Historical costumes of England 1066-1956*, Harrap, 1978
Brooke, Iris and Laver, James	*English costume of the eighteenth century*, Black, 1931
Braun-Ronsdorf, Margarete	*The wheel of fashion*, Thames and Hudson, 1964
Buck, Anne	*Dress in eighteenth century England*, Batsford, 1979
Bury, A. and Cammell, C.D.	*World famous paintings*, New Educational Press, 1958
Calthrop, Dion Clayton	*English costume*, Black, 1941
Cassin-Scott, Jack	*Costume and Fashion 1550-1760*, Blandford Press, 1971
Clarke, John	*The life and times of George III*, Weidenfeld & Nicolson, 1972
Cumming, Valerie	*Exploring costume history 1500-1900*, Batsford, 1981
Cunnington, C.W. & P.	*Handbook of English costume in the eighteenth century*, Faber, revised ed. 1972
Cunnington, C.W. & P.	*History of underclothes*, Faber, revised ed., 1981
Cunnington, Phillis & Buck, Anne	*Children's costume in England 1300-1900*, Black, 1965
Dymoke, J.	*London in the eighteenth century*, Longman 1958
Ewing, Elizabeth	*Everyday dress 1650-1900*, Batsford, 1984
Ewing, Elizabeth	*History of children's costume*, Batsford, 1977
Foster, Vanda	*Bags and purses*, Batsford, 1982
Halliday, F.E.	*Dr Johnson and his world*, Thames and Hudson, 1968
Hayes, John	*Gainsborough*, Phaidon, 1975
Holland, Vyvyan	*Hand coloured fashion plates 1770-1899*, Batsford, 1955
Laver, James	*Costume and fashion, a concise history*, Thames & Hudson, 2nd ed., 1982
Lister, Margot	*Costumes of everyday life*, Barrie and Jenkins Ltd, 1972
London, Museum	*Men's costume 1580-1750*, H.M.S.O., 1970
London, Museum	*Men's costume 1750-1800*, H.M.S.O., 1973
Pictorial Encyclopaedia of Fashion	Hamlyn, 1968
Power, E.G.	*A textile community in the industrial revolution*, Longman, 1969
Ribeiro, Aileen	*A visual history of costume in the eighteenth century*, Batsford, 1983
Ribeiro, Aileen	*Dress in eighteenth century Europe 1715-1789*, Batsford, 1984
Sichel, M.	*The eighteenth century* – costume reference series, Batsford, 1977
Taylor, Basil	*Stubbs*, Phaidon 2nd ed., 1975
Waugh, Norah	*Corsets and crinolines*, Batsford, 1954
Webster, Mary	*Hogarth*, Studio Vista, 1979
Williams-Mitchell, Christobel	*Dressed for the job*, Blandford Press, 1982
Wilson, Eunice	*A history of shoe fashion*, Pitman, 1974

Things to Do

1. Draw a picture of a young child dressed in the fashions of 1750. Beside this, draw a picture of a child of today. Compare their clothes. What are the major differences?

2. Design a fabric suitable for a rich lady or gentleman of the eighteenth century. Look at the pictures on pages 10, 24, 30 and 40 to help you. Make your design very elaborate and think about the colour of your material.

3. Find out all you can about eighteenth-century make-up. What were some of the harmful effects of the preparations that were used?

4. Find out as much as you can on eighteenth-century hairdressing. Look at all the different styles of wigs for men and the elaborate hairstyles for women, particularly in the 1770s and 1780s. Write about how unhygienic some of these styles must have been.

5. See if you can make a hoop petticoat or false hips with a friend. What would it have felt like to wear these all day long?

6. Try dressing up with your friends in eighteenth-century costume. Improvise where you can. Try making some false calves, false eyebrows and false hair pieces. How uncomfortable are they?

7. Compare the costumes of a rich family from this book with those of a poor family. Think very carefully about their clothes and the differences in material etc. Write about how the children from each family might have spent their day.

8. Find out about the accessories of fashionable people in the eighteenth century. In particular, gloves, fans, snuff boxes and canes. Draw pictures of them.

9. Find out more about the soldiers who fought for England in the American War of Independence. Draw some of their uniforms. How practical were they?

riding habit, c. 1785